MEMORIES OF THE DISPOSSESSED

Descendants of Kulak Families Tell Their Stories

Russian Memoirs Series No. 2

MEMORIES OF THE DISPOSSESSED

Descendants of Kulak Families Tell Their Stories

Personal histories collected by
Olga Litvinenko

Edited and translated with introductory chapters by
James Riordan

Bramcote Press
Nottingham

First published 1998 by
BRAMCOTE PRESS
Nottingham, England.

Printed in Great Britain by
Antony Rowe Ltd, Chippenham, Wiltshire

Cover design by MAM 0115 948 3344
Cover photograph from the Slava Katamidze Collection

British Library Cataloguing in Publication Data.
A catalogue record for this book is available from the British Library.

ISBN 1 900405 06 7

CONTENTS

CONTENTS

PREFACE

THIS BOOK consists of interviews with children, grandchildren and great-grandchildren of kulak farmers living in the Kurgan Region. Surrounded by such huge industrial centres as Yekaterinburg (Sverdlovsk) and Chelyabinsk, the Region may well seem relatively small. All the same, 45 percent of the rural population still supplies basic provisions to both the regional centre and many other Russian cities. At the turn of the century, Kurgan butter-makers even provided butter for Queen Victoria.

My interest in the dekulakization process is more than academic. For not only was I born and grew up in Kurgan, my great-grandmother and great-grandfather were among the kulak victims of collectivization. I learned this from my grandmother, although sadly she died before I realized the need to question her closely about it.

Even today Russia lags far behind the West in a proper study of collectivization. We could not even talk about the 1929-33 period before 1990, let alone write anything adverse about it. Imagine my surprise when I arrived in Britain and found several books on dekulakization published back in the 1970s!

All the same, I humbly present this book to the Western reader in the hope that the direct, personal stories of my respondents will complement the more sober, less impassioned studies of Western scholars.

Many descendants of dekulakized peasant farmers, especially the elderly, still fear to tell the truth about their past. Fear is the solitary legacy passed on from one generation to the next in peasant families. At their request, I give only the first names and letters of surnames of my interviewees. I keep the cassette recordings of their stories in my apartment in Kurgan, hoping that one day they will be part of a sound archive in Russia on a par with that in the West.

I would like to acknowledge my gratitude to all those who have in one way or another taken part in this book. First and foremost I would like to thank my co-author Professor James Riordan for his help in translating and annotating all the interviews, and for his support in my application for a British Academy grant to enable me to study at the University of Surrey. This made it possible for me to consult relevant literature and to work on the English version of the book.

I would also like to express my gratitude to Professor Daniel Bertaux at the Social Movement Study Centre in Paris. It was while working on a research project with him that I obtained much valuable information as well as funding for conducting my interviews.

I would also like to thank my Moscow colleagues, particularly Victoria Semyonova at the Institute of Sociology, and Ludmila Koklyagina of the Institute for Youth Studies, for their long-term moral and financial support. It would have been quite impossible to do such research in the provinces without their collaboration. I also owe a debt of thanks to Kurgan historians, archive assistants and my own students for their aid in locating the necessary information.

Finally, I wish to express my immense gratitude to my parents for taking care of my son while I was preparing this book.

Olga Litvinenko

AN OUTLINE OF RUSSIAN RURAL HISTORY
1861-1933

1861-1913

FOR A perspective on Russian history, it is salutary to remember
that in much of Western Europe the serf or manorial system of
farming lasted until the fourteenth or fifteenth centuries. The serf
was a farm labourer who could not be removed from the
squire's land on which the serf worked, and was transferred
with it when the land passed to another owner. In other words,
the serf belonged, like a slave, to his or her master.

In Russia, serfdom in its extreme form lasted until 1861. Yet
it did not extend over the entire Russian Empire; the southern
Urals and Siberia (dealt with in this book) were areas of free
farming. By 1861 about a third of the Russian population lived
in serf-free areas.

The Emancipation Act of 1861 was intended to retain the
power and privilege of the aristocratic landowners, staunch
allies of the monarchy, while granting peasants their personal
freedom. Many peasants actually regarded the Act as a betrayal,
for the amount of land they received was less than they had
cultivated for their own needs when they were serfs. Moreover,
they had to pay for that land, even though very few had any
money.

By the turn of the century, landowners retained some
100,000 estates, covering almost all the pastures and forests and
over half the arable land. Since the peasant population more
than doubled between 1861 and 1900, in economic terms (food
consumption and per capita income), the hundred million peasants were actually worse off in 1900 than the forty million
peasants had been in 1800. What is more, whereas the various
'enclosure acts' in Western Europe had 'freed' peasants to work
in the towns, the terms of the Emancipation Act made it very
difficult for the Russian peasant to leave his or her village and
to obtain a temporary internal passport from the police. The

1

peasants were the only social group without an automatic right to internal passports.

The Act therefore resulted in very little redistribution of land. Consequently, adult children with their families had to continue living with their parents, typically producing the extended Russian family with several generations living under one roof.

When Russia became the first European power in modern times to be defeated by an Asiatic state—in the 1904-5 Russo-Japanese War, the humiliating set-back led to many uprisings in urban centres. This '1905 Revolution' quickly spread to the countryside, and many thousands of 'nests of gentry' went up in smoke as peasants took revenge for the many centuries of cruel repression. A peasant war was fast developing.

Although the 1905 Revolution was ruthlessly suppressed, the Tsar realized that something had to be done to prevent an explosion in the countryside from destroying the old order. The result was the Stolypin reforms, whose principal objective was to encourage peasant migration from the overpopulated central provinces to the Urals and Siberia, and to break up the village commune (obshchina) in order to establish a new class of independent yeoman farmers.

Pyotr Stolypin became Prime Minister in July 1906; three days later, he issued a decree cancelling all peasant redemption debts, permitting the peasants to withdraw from the communes and offering grants to peasants wishing to settle in the Urals and Siberia. The newly-completed Trans-Siberian Railway made eastward movement much easier.

Stolypin himself did not live to see the results of the reforms: he fell victim to an assassin's bullet in 1910. All the same, his hope was fulfilled that a class of wealthy peasants would come into being. Agricultural production began to grow rapidly and the peasants became increasingly differentiated into social or class groups. Many peasants left the communes to start their own farms and formed a group known as middle peasants (serednyaki). And a wealthier group, known as kulaki (whom we shall henceforth refer to as 'kulaks'), came to possess their own family farms; some employed farm hands, some lent money or grain, leased farm machinery or mills. A third group of poor peasants (bednyaki) often preferred to sell or rent their strips of land and enter employment.

By 1913, on the eve of World War I, the kulaks were already producing more marketable grain than the landowners.

In the decade 1906 to 1916, their productivity was higher than that of both the landowners and the village commune.

Stolypin's reforms also accelerated the colonization of eastern Russia: about three million peasants settled in the eastern Urals and Siberia during this period. By average Russian standards, most of these peasants, as Dr Litvinenko attests, were relatively prosperous individual farmers or kulaks. There was plenty of land available and no problem of overpopulation.

1914-1917

When World War I started in August 1914, some fifteen million peasants were taken into the tsarist army. Despite the rapid growth in the wartime urban population, Russia was still a predominantly rural country: in 1917, some twenty-nine million people lived in towns and one hundred and thirty-five million were rural residents. As the war progressed and the Russian army retreated, farm production could not be expected sufficiently to feed the swollen cities and the vast army.

The February 1917 Revolution was a spontaneous, popular uprising primarily caused by the government's inability to provide food. The slogans were mostly 'Bread!', 'Down with the War!' and 'Down with the Tsar!'. The Tsar soon abdicated, leaving power to the Provisional Government or Duma. With the collapse of the monarchy and law and order, most of the landowners fled the towns or went abroad, thereby deserting their estates; this resulted in a mad scramble by the peasants to confiscate whatever land, equipment and possessions they could. It was a time to pay off old scores, as the Revolution's chronicler Leon Trotsky describes:

> It was time to finish them off. The movement overflowed its banks, swept through all areas, wiping out local differences, drawing in all peasant social groups, washing away all considerations of law and order, became a raging, furious torrent, arming itself with steel and fire...destroying and burning down the manors, driving out the landowners, cleansing the earth and, in some places, soaking it with blood...
>
> Old Russia went up in smoke...The Russian muzhik was fulfilling his progressive historic mission with the only means at his disposal. With revolutionary barbarism he was wiping out medieval barbarism. What is more, neither he,

nor his grandfather, nor his great-grandfather before him, had ever experienced any mercy or compassion.[1]

In 1917 Russia was experiencing a spontaneous peasant revolt; no political party played a significant role. While the Bolsheviks took power in the major cities by a palace coup (on 25 October 1917, old style) and issued a Decree on Land on 26 October, giving the nobility's land to the peasants, in fact no estate land was left to give; it had been already taken. All the Decree did was to acknowledge that a hundred and fifty million hectares of arable land, pastures and forests were now in the hands of twenty-five million individual peasant households.

1918-1926

The new Bolshevik government soon found itself faced with the painful task of having to feed the towns and the army, and therefore having forcibly to confiscate food from the peasants. This problem was aggravated by the fact that for its first four years in power, the new régime found itself embroiled in war—the final year of World War I and then Civil War against White Guard armies backed by foreign powers. It was this terrible dilemma that dictated its harsh policies towards the peasants in general, and the wealthier peasants in particular.

The Civil War (1918-21) created just as much a dilemma for the peasant. Whereas many middle and wealthy peasant farmers had lost confidence in the Bolsheviks, they often put even less trust in the White armies whose policy was basically to restore the landowning estates. Essentially, the peasant had to choose between two hostile forces: the Red or the White terror. In any case, the Civil War was destroying the normal pattern of rural life; human losses were enormous and were made worse by the ensuing famine of 1921-2, which was unprecedented in Russian history.

Although the government radically changed course in March 1921 (by which time the Bolsheviks had prevailed in the war over the White Guards and their British, United States, French and Japanese collaborators) to a New Economic Policy (NEP), it was too late to prevent widespread famine, and more than five

---

[1] Leon Trotsky, *History of the Russian Revolution,* vol. II (London: Sphere, 1967), p. 37.

million people died of malnutrition and starvation in the autumn and winter of 1921-2—in excess of the number who had died in the Civil War.

Under the new policy, the food requisitioning detachments were disbanded; the communes were turned into 'land associations'; the requisitioning was replaced by a tax in kind; power was transferred from the poor peasants and the revolutionary committees to the village councils (soviets) and the kulaks were encouraged to increase production and take on farm hands.

This helped to repair some of the damage done to kulak-Bolshevik relations. The first clash between them had occurred in the spring and summer of 1918 when the Bolsheviks had begun forcibly to confiscate surplus agricultural produce and give local power to the poor peasant committees. At that time, the Bolshevik leader Vladimir Lenin had insisted on all-out struggle against the kulaks:

> The kulaks are the implacable enemies of Soviet power. Either they will defeat the mass of workers, or the workers will mercilessly crush the risings of the rapacious kulak minority against the worker government.[1]

This was written, of course, when the fate of the régime was in the balance. Even so, at no time did Lenin call for expropriation of the kulaks and their families. He repeatedly stressed that the kulaks were not to be stripped of their property—unlike the landowners and capitalists. Part of what they produced was the fruit of their own labour. If they rebelled, they were to be put down, but they should not be expropriated. When planning NEP, Lenin's idea was that the kulaks would be gradually squeezed out by economic means: 'If you can equip the peasants with machinery, you will improve their lot, and when you add electrification, you will squeeze out hundreds of thousands of petty kulaks.'[2] Lenin died in January 1924. The next three decades were dominated by Joseph Stalin, and all developments in rural life reflected his policies.

---

[1] V.I.Lenin, *Polnoe sobranie sochineniy*, vol. 37 (Moscow: Politizdat, 1962) p. 41.

[2] *Ibid*, vol. 43, pp. 69-70.

During the first part of the 1920s the kulaks strengthened their economic position and influence—with official support. The question of their elimination was raised only by the most extreme left-wingers. Even in the Party press right up to 1928-1929 not one writer posed the question of forced expropriation and eviction of the kulaks. Their importance as a productive unit of the peasant community was officially acknowledged.

1927-1933

The tide began to turn in 1927 when the Party Central Committee started to prepare draft resolutions for the fifteenth Party Congress to be held in December. These resolutions envisaged the collectivization of agriculture, which was to be the chief aim of making the countryside socialist. The Congress itself introduced a graduated system of agricultural tax in kind, much higher for those classified as kulaks. Some restrictions were also imposed on the leasing of land and the employment of farm hands.

At the time, according to Congress figures, kulaks numbered less than four percent of all households, while accounting for some ten percent of overall farm production. The initial ideas of collectivization were to transform the land associations into peasant cooperatives; but it was expected that these cooperatives would coexist with private individual farming for some years to come. The Congress made clear that collectivization was to be based on complete freedom of choice.

After the Congress, however, a new campaign against kulaks gathered momentum in early 1928. In many regions, officials were instructed to begin redistributing land, confiscating the 'surplus' land of the better-off peasants. At the same time, Stalin demanded that local authorities take 'extraordinary measures' against peasants, especially kulaks who tried to hoard grain. A special article had been added to the Criminal Code by which hoarding grain for the purpose of speculation was deemed a criminal offence punishable by deprivation of freedom for up to three years and confiscation of property.

Consequently, the wealthier peasants began to cultivate less land and produce less. Furthermore, many of those who owned mills, smithies and other workshops (private enterprise encouraged by NEP) sold up and moved to the towns. Older family members tended to continue living in the villages, while the younger, able-bodied people were capable of finding jobs in the rapidly-developing industry. Previously it had been the poorest peasants who had left for the towns; now it was the more prosperous, efficient and able-bodied, their instinct for self-preservation driving them out. Like Timofei's younger brother in Victor M's story, they foresaw the anti-kulak crusade approaching and did not wish to remain in a hostile environment.

The reduction in farm production and exodus from the village resulted in a widespread grain shortage and bread rationing; it was threatening the success of the First Five-Year Plan which had been launched on 1 October 1928. The pace of industrialization was directly related to the state's ability to feed the increasing industrial population. Stalin had argued in November 1928 that it was absolutely essential for the Soviet Union to catch up and overtake the leading industrial nations of the West: 'Either we succeed or they will destroy us.'[1] By early 1929 a new offensive against the kulaks seemed inevitable.

In December 1929, a special Politburo commission on collectivization, as well as a sub-commission specifically on the kulaks, were formed. However, Stalin did not wait for their recommendations. Without any formal announcement, officials began to confiscate grain in the early spring of 1929; thousands of kulaks and middle peasants were arrested and their grain supplies were confiscated. The local militia was reinforced in the summer by large numbers of security police, special detachments of Communist Party and Young Communist (Komsomol) activists, who were despatched to the countryside, and as many as fifty thousand industrial workers who were sent from industrial centres to assist in the grain procurement. Many were armed (in the 1920s, communists and Komsomol activists were allowed to possess firearms, and often wore them ostentatiously in special belts).

As before, peasants tried to hide their harvested grain. But those caught concealing grain or speculating were arrested immediately. Many kulaks and middle peasants whose wealth was in farm animals, not in land or grain, hurriedly disposed of

---

[1] I V Stalin, *Works*, vol. 13 (Moscow: Foreign Languages Publishing House, 1954), pp. 40-41.

part of their livestock, slaughtering many cattle and pigs. 'Self-liquidation' on the part of the kulaks became even more widespread.

At the same time, a new onslaught on the churches and religion took place. The régime felt that the Church could act as a rallying point for peasant resistance to its large-scale collectivization plans. So activists, especially Komsomol members, raided village churches, looting and stripping them of icons and other religious objects, which were often burned. Church services were made illegal (this lasted until 1943 when the government realized that the Church could be a patriotic force in the war effort). In August 1928 the Party shut down the remaining rural monasteries, deporting the monks to Siberia and using the land for new collective or state farms, and their buildings for workshops, garages, silos or tractor stations. It was at this time that my wife's grandfather, a mullah in a Tatar village in Bashkiria, was arrested and taken away as a 'religious kulak'. He was never heard of again. His brother escaped into the hills, lived there for several years and only returned to his village in 1941 at the outbreak of war.

Although Stalin did not call for mass collectivization at once, he declared, on 7 November 1929, 'a determined socialist offensive against capitalist elements' and 'a radical transformation of our farming from small, backward, individual farming to large-scale, advanced, collective farming.'[1] Three days later, a special plenary session of the Party Central Committee expelled 'right-wingers' Rykov and Bukharin from the Politburo as 'defenders of the kulaks'. It also set quotas for collectivization in each region. The initial recommendations envisaged 30 to 40 percent collectivization in 1930 and 70 to 80 percent in 1931.

Although the Party recognized that the kulaks represented the most efficient and hard-working part of the rural population, the Politburo's attitude was clear: in the ultimate struggle to decide who will beat whom *(kto kogo?)*—the Bolsheviks and their 'socialist' collective farming or the kulaks and their private capitalist farming—the time had come for a showdown and the 'elimination of the kulaks as a class'. This was to require the arrest and deportation of some five to six million people!

---

[1] *Ibid*, vol. 12, p. 138 (the article was entitled 'A Year of Great Break-Through').

A plan was drawn up by the Special Subcommission on the Kulaks, dividing kulaks into three groups:

1. Kulaks who opposed collectivization and engaged in counter-revolutionary activity.
   These were to be arrested forthwith and exiled to remote regions (i.e. the Northern Urals and Siberia).

2. Kulaks who opposed collectivization, but did not engage in sabotage.
   These were to be resettled in regions outside their native areas (in practice in the underdeveloped or virgin lands of European Russia or Kazakhstan).

3. Kulaks who accepted collectivization and were loyal to the Soviet régime.
   These were to be permitted to join the collective farms, but deprived of voting rights for three to five years.

Stalin, however, did not accept the recommendations—particularly the admission of kulaks into the collective farms. On 27 December 1929, he declared his intention of destroying the kulaks:

> We have recently moved on from restraining the exploiting tendencies of the kulaks, embodied in the policy of eliminating the kulaks as a class...Now dekulakization...is an integral part of the development of the collective farms... When you cut off the head you don't mourn for the hair.[1]

The official Party ruling on dekulakization came on 30 January 1930, with a resolution on 'Measures to Eliminate Kulak Households in Areas of Full-Scale Collectivization'. An army of a million armed people was mobilized to destroy the kulaks. Temporary prisons and transit camps were hastily set up; a large number of prosecutors was sent to the countryside to give the operation a semblance of legality. In every district a special Dekulakization Commission was established to preside over a network of 'troika' boards—consisting of a local Party, a government and a security police chief. The troikas were to prepare lists of kulaks, with an inventory of their property and

---

[1] *Ibid*, p. 176.

livestock to be confiscated. All confiscated goods were to be transferred to the collective farms which were to be set up while dekulakization was under way.

This was a vicious, cruel campaign waged by Stalin under the 'class war' slogan, to exterminate every last peasant who stood in the way of mass collectivization. The use of the term 'kulak' had been a distortion of the truth right from 1917; but by now it was hardly applicable to any economic class. Many 'kulaks' even on Stalin's definition had been ruined by the late 1920s; and the remainder were hardly wealthy. Only one percent of all farms employed more than a single worker. The average kulak's income was in fact lower than that of the average rural official who was persecuting him as the representative of a well-to-do class!

In practice, the entire anti-kulak operation soon got out of hand, and embraced large numbers of peasants of every economic station: wealthy, middling and poor. Even a very poor peasant, if a devout believer, would be a kulak. A woman teacher, dekulakized on the grounds that she was a priest's daughter, 'produced documents that showed that she was the daughter of a peasant', whereupon 'they declared that "her mother had visited the priest, and therefore it was possible that she was the priest's daughter"'.[1] Such terrible and ridiculous stories are legion. As was officially stated, 'By "kulak" we mean the bearer of certain political attitudes which are most frequently evident in the subkulak.'[2] Thus, any peasant whatsoever was liable to dekulakization. Olga Litvinenko's stories amply bear this out.The dekulakization policy made little economic sense in that it led to the removal from the village of the most efficient producers. In political terms, however, it was intended to eliminate the natural leaders of the peasants against the communist subjugation of the rural population. Yet subsequent rural history does not bear out any short or long-lasting political success; just the opposite. The modern Russian writer Sergei Zalygin has written of collectivization in Siberia that 'the best peasants were deliberately wiped out; a rabble of idlers, windbags and demagogues came to the top; any strong

---

[1] See *Narodnoe prosveshchenie*, no 6, 1930, p. 17; quoted in Robert Conquest, *The Harvest of Sorrow* (London: Arrow, 1986), p. 131.

[2] *Na agrarnom fronte*, nos 7-8, 1930, p. 94. Quoted in Conquest, p. 119.

personalities were persecuted regardless of social background.[1] Another writer, Victor Astafiev, says that the dregs of society who came to power usually provoked the best peasants so as to get them sent to the camps.[2] The first arrests (in October-November 1929) consisted of heads of families, many of them former soldiers in White Guard armies. All were shot.

Then again, in December 1929, heads of families were taken, held in prisons for two or three months, then sent to camps. For the moment, their families were left untouched, though inventories were made of their property.

At the start of 1930, the families were rounded up.

It is hard to estimate how many 'kulaks' and their families were arrested and executed in the first wave. Official sources state that some two million people were deported; the actual number was probably much higher. The rate of collectivization was speeded up by the February 1930 dekulakization campaign and, in March, many regions reported that 70-80 percent of all households had been collectivized. Peasants had to offer their horses and cattle as a special entrance contribution. As a consequence, they demonstrated their resistance by slaughtering their livestock and poultry. In February 1930 alone some fourteen million head of cattle, a third of all pigs and a quarter of all sheep and goats were killed. Several million horses were also lost. This was a terrible disaster whose effects were to be felt for many years to come.

The authorities realized that the agricultural year would be utterly ruined unless something was done. On 2 May 1930, Stalin published his famous article in *Pravda*, 'Dizzy with Success', accusing local officials of engaging in arbitrary repression. The use of force was to cease at once and peasants were to be allowed to leave the collective farm if they so desired.

Stalin could never have foreseen the consequences of his announcement: by 1 July 1930 fewer than six million peasant households remained in the collective farms—i.e. about a quarter of all poor and middle peasants, 30 percent of the rural population. There had been a mass exodus. All the same, the

---

[1] Sergei Zalygin, 'Na Irtyshe,' in *Izbrannye proizvedeniya* (Moscow: Moskovskiy pisatel', 1973).

[2] Victor Astafiev, 'Posledniy poklon', *Roman-gazeta*, nos 2-3, 1979.

turn-round in policy did not help those already in a prison camp or on the way to deportation sites.

By the autumn of 1930, the voluntary principle of collectivization had not produced the desired results. So coercion was resumed, including dekulakization. The collectivization target figures were revised: 50 percent for the Urals, Siberia and Kazakhstan, and no less than 80 percent for the Ukraine, the Volga regions and the Northern Caucasus. This precipitated the second wave of dekulakization. In the first weeks of 1931, hitherto undeported kulaks failing to meet their quotas were expropriated and exiled. The formal decision on the second wave of deportation was taken in February 1931. Resistance was fiercest in the Urals, Siberia and the south of the country where the peasants had been free settlers for generations and were proud of their farming history. By 1931 more than 50 percent of the peasants in this region joined the collective farms, but they were poor peasants and relative newcomers to the area. The older residents were reluctant to join because they lived reasonably well and did not want to lose their freedom. The tragic stories related in this book confirm this.

Once again, the results of the dekulakization campaign were a reduction in state grain and meat deliveries, delayed sowing and harvesting, and the threat of starvation to both town and village. Inevitably, drastic measures were introduced. Resistance was once more put down to kulak sabotage. In fact, the conflict was now between the state and the collective farms: the new collective farmers *(kolkhozniki)* began to realize that, far from living better, they were actually worse off and now totally dependent on the state.

So they refused to work. They took the heads of grain for their own consumption and slaughtered their cattle and pigs (for which they had no fodder in any case).

Despite the new repressive measures the inevitable outcome was a new and terrible famine precipitated by the forced confiscation of all available grain. Peasants tried to move from village to town despite the road-blocks, military cordons and the reintroduction of the old tsarist passport system.

There are no official figures of the human cost of the man-made famine in 1932-1933. But unofficial estimates put it as high as five to six million lives, at least three million of whom were children. No mention of this famine—the worst in Russian history—was ever made officially until Nikita Khrushchev made his 'secret speech' at the twentieth Party Congress in 1956.

It was not until 8 May 1933 that an official end was called to the terror, in a secret 'Stalin-Molotov' missive sent to all Party and government workers, the security forces, the courts and prosecutors. By this time, however, the kulak in any sense whatsoever had been utterly wiped off the face of the Russian earth. All the same, police and activists carried on with their arrests and shootings regardless.

Russian and Western Scholars have calculated the death toll from collectivization and dekulakization roughly as follows:

Peasant dead: 1930-1937	11 million
Arrested and dying later in camps	3.5 million
TOTAL	14.5 million
Of these:	
Died as a result of dekulakization	6.5 million
Died in the Kazakhstan famine	1 million
Died in the 1932-33 famine	7 million

These figures are conservative estimates; they do not overstate the true situation.[1] The elimination of the kulaks, the forced collectivization of agriculture and the 1932-33 famine all had a huge and lasting impact on all aspects of life in Russia. This 'revolution from above', as Stalin called collectivization, radically changed the lives of the more than 80 percent of the Soviet population living in the countryside. It transformed an entire way of life—as, indeed, it was intended to do. Millions of peasant families were displaced and the whole process was enforced by a monstrous campaign of terror, deportation, exile and execution on an unprecedented scale.

That collectivization and dekulakization caused long-term damage to the countryside (eventually constituting a major contributory factor in the demise of the communist régime and the Soviet Union) is generally recognized today. A number of

---

[1]These estimates may be found in Conquest, p 306. Similar figures are to be found in Zhores Medvedev, *Soviet Agriculture* (New York: Norton, 1987), Roy Medvedev, *Let History Judge* (London: Oxford University Press, 1989), Moshe Lewin, *Russian Peasants and Soviet Power* (London: Oxford University Press, 1968), V.P.Danilov, *Sovetskaya dokolkhoznaya derevnya: naselenie, zemlepolzovanie, khozyaystvo* (Moscow: Nauka, 1977)

negative measures persisted for quite a long time. For example, the unpopular system of single annual payment in kind at the end of the agricultural season continued until the late 1950s (to be replaced by monthly cash payments); the arbitrary legal and police restrictions on peasant movement from village to village, and from village to town (associated with the non-issue of passports to collective farmers) survived until 1977.

The productivity of arable land and yields of main cereal crops stagnated until 1955; the total grain harvest, 86 million tonnes in 1913, remained at the same level until 1954; the number of livestock reached its 1928 level only in 1956.

Of course, the human cost of Stalin's rural policies was immeasurably higher. The terror used against millions of 'kulaks' and other peasants created an irreparable rift between the rulers and the ruled, and it dealt a decisive blow to agriculture by removing, as one writer puts it, 'the hardest working, the thriftiest and most progressive farmers in the village.'[1] Even a security police report in 1931 admits that 'the best and hardest workers of the land are being taken away, with misfits and loafers staying behind.'[2] As the respected Russian author Ilya Ehrenburg put it back in 1934, 'Not one of them was guilty of anything; but they belonged to a class that was guilty of everything.'[3]

---

[1] Maurice Hindus, *The Great Offensive* (New York, 1933), p 270.

[2] Quoted in Merle Fainsod, *Smolensk under Soviet Rule* (Cambridge, Mass., 1958), p. 250.

[3] Ilya Ehrenburg, *The Second Day*, quoted in Anatoly Goldberg, *Ilya Ehrenburg* (New York, 1984), p. 141.

Calendar of Major Events Affecting Farming, 1861-1933

1861	Emancipation of Serfs
1904-5	Russo-Japanese War (ending in Russian defeat)
1905	First Russian Revolution and stirrings of peasant revolt
1906	Stolypin agricultural reforms launched
1914	Start of First World War
1917 (Feb.)	Second Russian Revolution; abdication of Tsar
1917 (Oct.)	Third Russian Revolution and Bolshevik coup; Decree on Land (26 Oct.), acknowledging transfer of estate land to peasants
1918-21	Civil War: Red v. White Guards and foreign armies
1921 (Mar.)	New Economic Policy launched
1921-2	Mass famine: some five million starve to death
1924 (Jan.)	Lenin dies
1927 (Dec.)	Fifteenth Party Congress takes place: decides to industrialize rapidly and collectivize agriculture (based on freedom of choice)
1928 (Feb.)	Extraordinary measures against grain hoarders; confiscation of 'surplus' kulak land; many wealthy peasants move to towns
1928 (Aug.)	New onslaught on churches: church services made illegal; rural monasteries closed; monks and priests deported
1928 (Oct.)	First Five-Year Plan launched: priority to heavy industry
1929 (Apr.)	Stalin's campaign forcibly to procure grain; arrest of thousands of kulaks; despatch of activists to countryside

1929 (Nov./Dec.)	Stalin's 'determined socialist offensive' against the kulaks; setting new quotas for collectivization; 'elimination of kulaks as a class'
1930 (Jan.)	Party resolution on 'Measures to Eliminate Kulak Households'; establishment of dekulakization commissions and 'troika' boards
1929-30	Slaughter of cattle and destruction of crops
1930 (Mar.)	Stalin's 'Dizzy with Success' article: curbs use of force and allows free exodus from collective farms *(kolkhozy)*
1930 (July)	Only 30 percent of peasants remain in kolkozy
1930 (Oct.)	Coercion and mass collectivization resumed
1931 (Feb.)	Second wave of mass dekulakization
1931 (Apr.)	'Grain strikes' by collective farmers and more cattle slaughter
1932-3	Famine: 5-6 million die
1933 (May)	Stalin-Molotov letter calling an end to terror.

BACKGROUND TO THE TRANSURALS REGION

Pre-Revolution

THE KURGAN Region is also known as the Transurals, insofar as it lies immediately beyond the Ural Mountains. The area began to be colonized in the late sixteenth century, during the reign of Tsar Ivan the Terrible. Bands of Cossacks under Yermak doggedly fought to push eastwards the non-Russian half-nomadic, half-settled inhabitants of the area. Once they had cleared the territory, it was settled in two ways: voluntarily and forcibly. Peasants from the European part of Russia came of their own accord in search of free land, while criminals and unreliable 'politicos' were exiled there. The tsarist authorities regarded the place as a moderately severe punishment zone.

A distinguishing feature of the Region was that it never experienced serfdom, unlike the European part of Russia, where serfdom survived until 1861. The availability of free land enabled anyone, even exiles, to start up their own farm. The Transurals climate is severely continental, which means that the average July temperature is 18°C, with a maximum of 25-30°C, and the average January temperature is -18°C, falling to a minimum of -25 to -30°C. Snow lingers from mid-January until mid-April. Winter therefore lasts about six months.

The cultivation of new land in such inclement conditions required people not only to be extremely fit, but to be hardworking and tenacious. The weak would not survive.

The traditionally large peasant family was a matter of necessity owing to high infantile mortality: four or five children out of ten would normally survive. Through this natural selection process a social community had grown up by the late nineteenth century that knew no servitude, was physically tough and materially self-sufficient. Despite the freezing winters, the land was fertile, the forest rich in edible fungi and berries, and the rivers were teeming with fish. This enabled peasant farmers both to feed their large families and to have a surplus for market.

In summertime, the farmers grew wheat, rye, oats and various grasses for cattle feed. But even of a long winter evening no one would sit idle. The women would spin yarn and weave canvas clothing and matting on special weaving frames. The men would fish through the ice, repair farm equipment and find plenty of jobs about the house to keep them busy. The stove needed regular fuel, the cattle and poultry had to be looked after, and the handmade clothes all needed washing and rinsing in the icy streams. Villagers would make special ice holes for fishing and rinsing clothes. No job would be unaccompanied: there would be lots of songs, sad and happy, all beautifully tuneful and skilfully sung.

Almost all Russian peasant farmers were religious. Every largish village had its church, normally located on the highest elevation so that its gilded cupolas would be seen for miles around. Religion strictly regulated village life, alternating holy festivals with fasts when it was forbidden to eat meat or fish and to have sexual intercourse. The strictest feast, known as Lent or the Grand Fast, lasted about two months and culminated in the big church festival known as the Resurrection (Easter). Most churches had parish schools where village children could learn to read. The Bible was the first and only book read in village families, usually serving as a sort of manual on ethics, in the sense that it contained fundamental moral principles—like the Ten Commandments, which set the tone for everyday life.

Not all villagers prayed in church. A large number of Old Believers—about one quarter of the population—lived in the Kurgan Region, far more than in other Urals regions. These were people who had opposed liturgical reforms initiated by Patriarch Nikon in 1652-3. They attended special prayer houses and were popularly known as the 'two fingers' people, inasmuch as they crossed themselves with two instead of three fingers. The Land Commission statistics from the population census noted in the late nineteenth century that Old Believers were sober, modest and diligent people. As a rule, they distanced themselves from other peasant farmers and their villages were more prosperous and well-kept.

Village houses were usually wooden-built and surrounded by a high fence; three or four generations would often live in the same house, with the building normally divided into two and having two separate entrances. When the eldest son married, he took over the other half of the house and only later, when he had become independent, did he build his own home. A direct link between generations was maintained, first by strict social control, and second by care of one's elderly parents.

The first general census took place in Tobol'sk Province in 1897; it covered Kurgan Region and ten other areas. Of the 260,000 inhabitants of the Kurgan Region, 96 percent lived in the countryside. This was the social structure according to the 1897 figures:

1. Gentry	677 persons
2. Clergy	886
3. Merchants	312
4. Urban middle class (*meshchane*)	5,060
5. Foreigners	14
6. Peasants	252,049
7. Others	1,097
TOTAL	**260,095**

Russians dominated the ethnic make-up of the Region—some 99 percent; the rest comprised a sprinkling of Jews (regarded in Soviet society as a 'nationality'), Germans and Poles. The indigenous population—members of Siberian tribes—had long since been squeezed out.

At the time Kurgan itself was a small provincial town with 11,197 inhabitants, of whom 7,356 were *meshchane*, 3,493 exiles, 222 gentry, 71 clergy and 55 merchants. The town had only six streets, and the tallest building was the fire station. The town's chief point of interest was the Tobol River on whose left bank stood a white-stone church around which the principal town buildings were scattered. The right-hand, lower bank of the River, was uninhabited since it formed a vast meadowland. The 1897 census reported:

'The town's appearance on entering it from the Tobol Highway is quite imposing. Generally, Kurgan's exterior is pleasing, the streets are straight and broad, and the buildings are fine.'

The town could boast six educational establishments, public libraries and theatres. Since the bulk of the townspeople was made up of peasant farmers, the shops and markets sold fairly inexpensive produce: a pood (16.3 kilograms) of wheat flour cost 12 kopecks, a pound of beef cost 0.5 kopecks, a goose—

seven kopecks, ten eggs—1.5 kopecks, and a pail of milk—14 kopecks. At that time, a man engaged in fieldwork might earn a total of 70 to 80 kopecks a month, and a woman 40 to 50 kopecks.

At the end of the nineteenth century the tsarist government decided to commence construction of the Great Siberian Railway, to a distance of over eight thousand kilometres. It was an extraordinarily arduous undertaking: the navvies had to toil for fifteen to sixteen hours a day, up to their knees in snow, wearing light clothing and patched-up birch-bark footwear. Soldiers, exiles and Cossacks formed the bulk of the workforce. Their tools were primitive: axe, saw, spade and wheelbarrow. They had to saw through trees, root out tree stumps and possess immense stamina to survive the extreme Urals and Siberian climate day in day out. The project was finally completed in 1904, having involved a total of ninety thousand workmen.

It took two years for the track to cover the Kurgan Region. The railway had evidently been intended to go in a straight line to Siberia, eastwards from Mishkin Station, bypassing Kurgan. But on the initiative on the Kurgan merchant Dmitri Smolin, it not only went through the town, it even passed his own house, even though such construction was inconvenient and expensive. Kurgan merchants donated some one hundred thousand roubles in bribes to the construction chiefs and treated them to a sumptuous reception in the town. That clinched the deal.

Revolution and Dekulakization

Most peasants did not welcome the October Revolution of 1917, not because of any monarchist sympathies. Rather they saw the revolution as a natural disaster akin to a drought or hurricane. The dislocating events of the 1918-21 Civil War interrupted their work and way of life. By popular repute, they were robbed equally by Red and White armies. Evidently, Transurals farmers were politically indifferent and had no wish to take sides in the political struggle.

The 'building of socialism' in the Russian villages of the 1920s started with the introduction of exorbitant taxes and the fixing of a low state purchase price for grain. The Bolsheviks used young men and women from urban areas, dedicated to communist ideas, to suppress any countryside rebellion. In addition, children were taught to inform on their parents and neighbours to the authorities. Many of them were taken in by slogans and high-sounding phrases, and were unaware of the immorality of their actions. The consequences were the utter degradation of the countryside and a total food crisis.

In 1929 the Kurgan Region did not meet the farm production plan for many items. Prosperous farmers were afraid to sow, the medium farmers (the *'serednyaki'*) sowed only enough to support their own families, and poor peasants, as usual, believed that the Soviet authorities would help and protect them. Town-dwellers had been given ration coupons which went some way to regulating food distribution. But it was not enough, according to Communist Party archives, to prevent mounting anti-Soviet sentiments in both town and country. In order to avoid anti-Soviet demonstrations and to feed the workforce, the communists decided to collectivize peasant households.

There were no sound economic reasons for collectivization. The organization of collective farms was a *political* act which at once transformed the peasant owner and master of his property into a state serf. At least the authorities would not have to compel the peasants to hand in their grain, since the collective farm *(kolkhoz)* was the most convenient agent for all manner of manipulation and plunder.

On Stalin's initiative in 1929, the authorities proclaimed the slogan of total collectivization. In his article, 'Year of Great Change', Stalin averred that if we 'step up the rate' of kolkhoz expansion, 'our country will become one of the world's biggest grain-producing nations within some three years, perhaps the largest grain-producing power in the world.'

Since the communists were unable to interest peasant farmers economically, they resorted to all kinds of coercive measures to force them into the kolkhozy, including shooting, eviction and complete confiscation of property. The rate of collectivization was totally dependent on punitive measures. Scared by the coercive registration of kolkhoz membership, the peasant farmers hastily began to slaughter their cattle, sell for a pittance the property they had accumulated over the years and flee to the town. It was at this point that the authorities began to brand prosperous farmers and all kolkhoz opponents as kulaks (in Russian 'kulak' means a 'fist'—hence the 'tight-fisted one').

Despite all efforts, collectivization moved ahead at a sluggish rate, so that by 1 January 1930 only 30 percent of Kurgan Region peasant households were in collective farms, by contrast to 20 percent in the USSR as a whole.

The violence and arbitrary actions accompanying collectivization provoked strong resentment among peasant farmers. A number of areas witnessed peasant uprisings and even armed battles which necessitated troops to put them down.

In an attempt to quell peasant resistance once and for all, the Party Politburo passed a resolution in January 1930 on 'the total elimination of kulak farms'. Local Soviet agencies were given the right to resort to any means necessary to deal with the kulaks, up to and including the confiscation of their property and their expulsion from the area. The resolution categorized prosperous peasant farmers as follows:

> *Category One:* active kulaks who had taken part in uprisings; these were to be arrested forthwith and incarcerated without trial.
> *Category Two:* the most prosperous kulaks; these were to be exiled to thinly-populated areas in the northern Urals.
> *Category Three:* the remaining kulaks; these were to be resettled to poor land on the periphery of the region.

Each category had set control figures that could not be altered. The property of kulaks in Category One was to be totally confiscated. Category Two could retain only the bare necessities, a minimum of provisions and 500 roubles for travel to their place of exile. Kulaks in Category Three were permitted to keep a minimum of farm tools and household goods for farming on the new site.

Dekulakization took a vicious and headlong turn as if it were a wartime measure. Posters went up in all districts proclaiming 'Death to the Single Farmer!' and 'All Poor and Medium Peasants into Kolkhozy!' In order to fulfil the plan in any real sense, district chiefs had to dekulakize both medium peasant farmers and even some poor peasants.

They often took everything a peasant owned, even the bare necessities. According to figures from the Kurgan Region archives, 'the authorities confiscated even the last items of underwear, babies' nappies, feeding bottles and baby food.' Families were driven out half-naked into the freezing cold. Confiscated goods frequently got divided up among commission members. Documents of the time reveal that 'kulaks were arrested and stripped, and had their decent clothing exchanged for tattered rags; they lost their sheepskin coats, fur coats, hats and gloves.' The chairman of one rural council reported that commission members had gold rings on each finger. Thus, dekulakization turned into naked marauding.

On the estimates of Kurgan historians, between 1930 and 1932 as many as forty thousand peasant homesteads were destroyed in the Kurgan Region—that is, some 15 percent of all homesteads. If we consider that a typical family comprised between six and eight persons or more, some three hundred thousand people must have suffered repression—i.e. about one in five people.

The cost of this 'Year of Great Change' amounted to some 750,000 head of cattle; as a consequence, the rural economy was reduced to such a pitiful state that the repercussions are still being felt today. For example, average per capita meat consumption was nineteen kilograms in 1926, but only seven kilograms in 1931.

The collectivization policy resulted in terrible starvation throughout Russia in 1933; many peasants died right outside their homes; the streets were littered with corpses. Yet, at the same time, Stalin was exporting grain, thereby demonstrating the resounding success of collectivization. In fact, the kolkhoz harvest was two or three times less than that planned; so the state forcibly confiscated all grain, even that put by for seed. Kolkhoz chiefs reported back to the centre that 'The peasants are being forced to feed on dead animals, even rats. Labourers are toppling over into the furrows from exhaustion and hunger.' The historian V. Danilov estimates that between three and four million people died from starvation in Russia; the figure for the Kurgan Region has not yet been established.

Stalin pinned the blame for the starvation on kolkhoz chiefs and low-ranking Party organizations. In an attempt to escape from crisis, the Party made certain concessions, passing a law in 1935 to enable peasant farmers to own their own subsidiary allotments of no more than 0.6 hectares and a small number of cattle. The abundant harvests of 1936 and 1937 provided an opportunity to claw some concessions back. Kolkhoz members, however, continued to toil for the state for next to nothing. Payment was made according to the number of 'labour days' worked; yet labour days were related to the results of one's work. What is more, labour days were paid mainly in grain—from óne to two kilograms depending on the harvest. On average a kolkhoznik might accumulate some 200 labour days over a year. By contrast with urban dwellers, peasant farmers had no passports and were effectively tied to their collective farms like serfs.

In the late 1930s life in the Transurals village was subordinate to satisfying 'civilized' needs: the kolkhozy were obliged not only to deliver produce to the towns, they had to provide gratuitous labour for building roads and timber cutting. At the same time, the state began to carry out organized recruitment of collective farmers for work at industrial enterprises. For many young farmers this was the only way to leave the countryside; so they often willingly signed up for work and went off to a Young Communist building site.

Historians have studied the wartime and postwar periods of village development much better than prewar, and we do not touch upon them in this book. The interviews provide a detailed personal, first-hand account of peasant life in the Transurals and of the destinies of the people who lived there.

Dedicated to my son Andrei,
in the hope that he will
never have to endure the
suffering of his forbears.

Olga Litvinenko
Kurgan, 1994

VICTOR M

VICTOR M lives in Yekaterinburg. He was 77 in 1993. Thus, he was 13 at the time of the dispossession. As part of a kulak family he was sent into exile, survived all the horrors of those years, always recalling his father's words on his deathbed: 'Everything that happened to us is nothing more than sheer tyranny, a crime against humanity. You'll find out for yourself if you survive. I shall not.'

Victor did survive. He lived to a time in Russian history when the whole truth could be told. Because by this time he was almost totally deaf, it was difficult to talk to him. At my request, he wrote down his reminiscences which are given below. He had come to Kurgan in the hope of rehabilitating his parents. Learning of my search for material on 'dekulakization', he suddenly turned up one day at my Institute. That was in September 1993.

Although Russia does not yet have a law on compensation for loss or return of property to the victims of collectivization, Victor is still hoping for the return of his house. He dreams of spending his remaining days in his parents' cottage and dying in the village where he spent his childhood. He has been to look at the house on several occasions and has even made the acquaintance of the woman living there. He doesn't want to see any return of repression; so he would gladly accept part of the house without the present occupants being evicted.

Victor's story

Ik Village

The village of Ik where I was born in 1916 stood on both sides of a lake formed by a dam blocking a small river of the same name. According to my eldest sister Grapa, all four of us brothers were born in the bathhouse in the yard, close to the yard gate. I well remember that bathhouse where I often had to go to wash and steam myself.

In line with the then administrative division, Ik came within the vast Tobol'sk Province in Kurgan District, some sixty kilometres from the city of Kurgan, at the very margin of Russia and Siberia. The border passed close by the village estates. The present Guberl Village, four kilometres from Ik, was half Russian, half Siberian: the border passed through the main street and cut the village in two.

Once upon a time, so the story goes, a peasant from that village, residing on the Russian side of the street, committed some misdemeanour and was sentenced to Siberian exile. With the aid of some fellow villagers, he moved his house overnight to the other side of the street, where he could start his exile in Siberia!

I learned about our distant relatives on my father's side from aunts and uncles who have long since gone to rest in the village graveyard. The most distant known relative was a man by the name of Timofei Malkov. According to rough estimates he was born in the late eighteenth or early nineteenth century, and lived somewhere in central Russia, probably in the Moscow region, since quite a few native Muscovites and Moscow region inhabitants bear the surname Malkov.

Timofei's son Ivan was exiled to Siberia for some offence against the authorities, and he settled in Ik; he was possibly one of the first inhabitants of this Siberian hamlet.

Ivan Timofeich had two sons—Ustin Ivanich and Vasiliy Ivanich, who were born in the village itself and, naturally, bore the surname Malkov. Vasiliy did not live long: he fell ill and died of cholera, leaving two small children—Stepan and

Vasiliy—who were then eight and ten years old respectively. His brother Ustin took responsibility for bringing them up, even though he had five children of his own. So our granddad had to cope with seven kids.

That was at the end of the last century. According to relatives, our grandfather Ustin Ivanich died sometime between 1903 and 1905 at about the age of fifty, thereby bequeathing his wife a large family to support. But our grandmother Agafia Nikolaevna was a tough old woman who maintained a tidy household, keeping a tight rein on her numerous children.

The Big Family

By 1922 Grandma's family had grown: three of her sons—Mikhail, Kirill and Ivan—were already married, while two sons and the two daughters were still single.

All four brothers—three with families and the single brother—lived in the same house, wooden of course, comprising three rooms. The number of people under the same roof was twenty. You can imagine what it was like to live in the house. Yet they got on well together. The brothers hardly ever had a cross word; their strict grandmother Agafia Nikolaevna saw to that. On the other hand, the brothers' wives, especially those of Kirill and Ivan, had such strong characters that not even the all-powerful mother-in-law could reconcile them. Our mother with her large brood had the most difficult time of it. There were seven of us: three sisters and four brothers. I recall that our family of nine lived in a tiny room of no more than fifteen square metres. The other two rooms were much bigger, but they were taken up by Kirill's and Ivan's families, even though there were fewer of them. The men in those families were under their wives' heels...As far as our family was concerned, living conditions were quite unbearable. My mother was always on at my father to leave this hell-hole and take lodgings somewhere.

Once I remember Father telling my tearful mother, 'Hang on, lovey, my brothers are to build a separate house for our family. As soon as we build it we'll all move into a new house; for the time being we'll go and live with Grannie Sychishka.'

No one could explain to me who this Grannie Sychishka was, though I well recall living with her. We stayed there three long years before moving house; when we finally moved in 1925 the house had a roof, but was barely finished. Kirill's and

Ivan's families stayed behind in the old house; so did Timofei the elder for a time.

As well as the house we had a barn, a cowshed and a few cattle and an outhouse. The bath house was put up later. Our family therefore became sort of independent. But the independence was relative: the brothers did their farming jointly; so most of the cattle, mainly the cows, were kept at the new house, while the horses were stabled at the old house.

All the same, we were now separated from the communal family and lived our lives by ourselves—but not beyond the power of Grandmother Agafia Nikolaevna. She was always in and out of our new house, bringing the odd bits and pieces to our mother and giving Dad various instructions. At that time, in 1925, he was 45. Despite everything, a fair new life began for our family and we kids had a happy childhood.

My Father's Brothers

Let me try to describe each brother, what they did for a living, where they continued to live a communal life and where Agafia Nikolaevna still held undisputed sway. Let me start with the eldest, Mikhail, that is our father.

From time immemorial the inhabitants of our little Siberian village of Ik have been farmers, tilling the soil, husbanding cattle, utilizing what the local forest provided and the pastures around the village gave in the way of grazing land for the village cattle. By the late 1920s the village, consisting of about a hundred and twenty homesteads, had three large herds of cows. When I was last in my home village, in 1984, it had about twenty houses, only three recently constructed, and the rest were tumbledown shacks scattered over the former territory of the entire village.

Our family, headed by Father, was responsible for all manner of farming chores: we ploughed and sowed, we reaped and mowed, we kept cattle and were thoroughly content with that. At crucial times of seasonal work all the brothers and their wives lent a hand, with the sole exception of my mother whose job it was to make the meals for field and home. Of course, everything that we grew belonged to the large family as a sort of coöperative. We children worked with a will at all jobs; and when it came to horses, not a single horse-drawn job was done without us.

In the early part of the 1920s when the New Economic Policy was brought in, mainly to restore farming destroyed by the Civil War, the country was concerned to equip peasants with what new techniques there were, especially for bringing in the harvest. Such machinery was largely of American make. Our father and his three brothers clubbed together to purchase a Deering binder (principally for our family). Other homesteads had McCormick machinery. If you didn't have enough cash to buy a binder, you bought cheaper machines like reapers. The name speaks for itself: while the machine moved over the field, the cut stalks would fall on to a special platform which had to be constantly cleared. The person set to clean the platform had to work fast and soon worked up a sweat; so we used to call the reapers 'head-heaters'. There was other machinery called 'wings'; these wings would cast off the cut stalks from the platform as the machine shifted forward.

I have to say at this point that all questions concerning farming were decided collectively by the brothers and they did what suited them all. So the allocation of jobs among them depended on the skills each had built up throughout his lifetime.

The second eldest after Mikhail was Kirill. In his time free from farm work he was given the job of doing the village mechanical repairs.

All the farm machines and the village transport—carts, wains and so on—needed greasing. At that time the government was unable to supply villagers with enough greasing materials from petroleum products. So we had to think something up locally. Our Uncle Kirya, as we used to call him, had been all over Russia, serving in the Tsar's army and had seen ways of processing pitch from pine resin of long-dead trees. That's why he suggested doing the job for his brothers; naturally, the brothers readily agreed and he was responsible for such chores.

At the suggestion of the brothers, the local authority set aside a clearing in the pinewood nearby for a special roofed-in forge. Close by the forge stood a little hut for staying overnight. It even had a small garden where mainly potatoes grew so that they didn't have to be carried from home. Everyone called the forge and hut our 'factory'. I describe the 'factory' from memory, as I saw it when I first went there; I later visited it often.

The hardest thing about tar extraction was getting hold of the resin; that was a burden for all the brothers. The trouble was that you had to dig up old roots of pine trees in which the resinous substance had accumulated.

Besides pitch, Uncle Kirya used to make pure tar from birch bark (bast) at his 'factory'; he'd use this for leather footwear; some people even bought Kirill's products for medicinal purposes. All the 'factory's' products were snapped up within the village, though sometimes they went to market in the town of Kurgan.

All that I've described so far was confined to the summer season. You have to remember that we also had the long Siberian winter. We had to do something in the wintertime and not sit there twiddling our thumbs to while away the time: it lasted six months of the year, after all. What is more, apart from wheat, oats, rye, barley and other cereals, the peasants also sowed flax, hemp and poppy. The first two basically served a sort of cottage industry for women to make good quality cloth from which they would sew both underclothes and outer garments: state garment mills weren't a patch on our peasant garment-makers.

Out of the flax and hemp we had not only cloth, but seeds as well. Every peasant farmer was concerned about the future harvest and so put by the necessary seeds he needed. Most of the seeds were, however, left over for other uses. Our father and his brothers would sweep up these 'spare' seeds and had permission to operate an oil press. That one could make oil from seeds was long known in the countryside. I read somewhere that it was a Voronezh peasant who first made the discovery. The brothers handed the job over to Kirill once more and he was a dab hand at it. Incidentally, the business had been running since before the Revolution. For the peasant folk of many neighbouring villages, not to mention our village, this oil production was a real bonus. Throughout the winter, one after the other, they used to arrive at our house, queuing up for the stuff. After completing the cycle, the customers used to collect up oil cake as well for their animals. They would pay cash for the work.

The technology of oil processing required certain rotating and twisting mechanisms which, naturally enough, were operated by horse power. And wherever there were horses, as I have said, you would find us kids.

Another of the younger brothers, Uncle Vanya, also did a useful job for his fellow villagers. I have already mentioned that we had three big herds of cattle in our small village. There was not a single farmyard which did not have its share of cattle—cows, pigs, sheep and goats. In autumn, each farmstead would slaughter just about everything apart from the poultry. The meat went to feed the family or got sold at market, but the hides mostly used to go to waste, as they were beyond the existing peasant technology. So they were generally sold cheaply at market or were chucked out. My father and his brothers were well aware of this waste. So at a village council one day they decided to try to process the hides—the job was allotted to the youngest brother, Uncle Vanya. And Uncle Vanya did what he could, with help from his brothers. To start with he would work only on the hides of our own cattle; but when he got the hang of it he used to take orders from other villagers. Now and again, whenever they used horses for providing extra elbow grease, they could not get by without us kids.

So this was how first four, then three brothers—the family cooperative—lived until the winter of 1929.

Tragedy

Autumn 1929. All the major farming jobs were over: the corn was harvested and threshed, the logs had been cut and carted home, the cattle sheds had been prepared; I, Alexander and Grigoriy had started a new term at school—for all peasant folk it was time to 'rest' from the onerous summer labours. The previous autumn, in 1928, Father's brother, Timofei the younger, had paid us a visit to see his brothers—for the last time, as it turned out; by that time he had completed his college course and was teaching at a forestry institute somewhere in Kazakhstan.

He was well acquainted with the recent Fifteenth Party Congress and its decisions to collectivize agriculture and, on that basis, to eliminate the kulaks as a class. None of the peasant farmers, including my father and his brothers, had wind of that or, as events were to show, wished to know anything about it. All the same, Timofei realized what it all would mean. Our father and his brothers Kirill and Ivan, despite having their family responsibilities, were not very far-sighted, although one could not call them illiterate or unread. They certainly used to read the *Red Kurgan* paper that we subscribed to and which invariably carried news of the Congress. They had no wish to listen to their learned brother who had advised them to throw everything up and quit the village, moving as far away as possible and finding work in the town. (We now know that many peasant farmers did just that—packed it in, boarded up their houses, went off to town and joined the ranks of the working class.) To all the urgings of his brother, my father would say,

'Where am I to go with this horde of kids?'

By 'horde of kids' he meant his four sons, the eldest of whom, Alexander, was only fifteen at the time. They, my father and his brothers, gave no thought even to dividing things up properly among themselves, even though they had their different families.

One evening in December 1929—it turned out to be the most miserable day of all—a terrible tragedy befell our household. My eldest brother Alexander came rushing into the house out of breath and terribly upset; he called father into the next room for some secret conversation. He obviously was bringing urgent news if he could not tell the rest of us. When they came back into the room, my father and brother sat at the table. Mother went and sat down beside them. Since we were not yet asleep, we lifted up the curtain to look at the table where my parents and Alexander were sitting and whispering, evidently something to do with the news my brother had brought.

I will never forget that soon after, the unlocked door opened and into the house came two men with hunters' guns in their hands; they sat down next to my brother, shoving him to the end of the bench. Where had they appeared from? Why had they come to us? Why had they walked in uninvited?

It was not until sixty years later, in 1989, that my brother confided in me what had transpired on that fateful night. He was fifteen then; he was now 76. This is what he wrote to me from Kurgan:

'Vitya, you may well remember that Tatiana Gasnikova's family lived next door to us; she had four children, two sons and two daughters. Her husband had died back in 1919 or 1920. Tatiana's children were the same age as us: Grigoriy was my age, Ivan was yours, while their sisters, Darya and Alexandra, were the same age as our younger brothers Grigoriy and Fyodor. All our childhood games involved Tatiana's children, although our new house had no place for playing games. They, though, had a big grassy yard which we village kids used to call our meadow. We played together in winter as well as summer.

'One winter's day, exactly when I don't remember, I was playing with Tatiana's children, Grigoriy and Ivan when I heard them talking about some very important meeting of villagers that was to be held in our school. The meeting had been called for all men and women of the village poor. I had not given much thought then to the fact that Grisha's mum was going to the meeting. Turning to me, Grishka had said: 'Let's go to school and hear what the meeting has to say.'

'So we trooped along behind his mother. And when they did not let us into the school, that only roused our interest in the meeting. Our first thought was: where could we hide ourselves to find out what was going on?

'After all the assembled guests had made their way into the school, Grishka, Vanka and I slipped in through the doors and hid under the platform that had evidently been knocked together specially for the meeting. We sat hidden underneath the stage right to the end of the meeting and heard everything that was said. Even as we were approaching the school building we noticed Semyon Yezhov (nicknamed the 'Hedgehog'— *Yozhik*) and some unfamiliar fellow in a leather jacket welcoming the peasant farmers into the school hall; they had barred our way.

'It was Semka the Hedgehog who opened and conducted the meeting; he was the Young Communist League organizer in the village. Semka introduced this other fellow, apparently some bigwig from the local district centre. From his very first words it was clear he was referring to our resettlement—i.e. in line with the dekulakization policy: how many families the district office had put on the rota. I had heard about this dekulakization at school, but I had no idea what it was.

'A discussion commenced on our village muzhkiks, when and by whom they had been put on the lists demanded by the district Party Committee. When our father's turn came, Semka the Hedgehog told the meeting,

'We must dekulakize Malkov, Mikhail Ustinovich and his sons Kirill and Ivan!'

Someone hollered from the hall,

'Kirill and Ivan are Mikhail's brothers, not his sons!'

Then the stranger, who had been standing by the table, broke into the discussion:

'For a more weighty resolution of this issue, let us act as follows: we'll make the eldest brother, Mikhail, father of his younger brothers and dekulakize all three at once as a single family unit; we'll remove them from the meeting's minutes. No one's going to check anyway; that way we'll have carried out the Party district committee's instructions. If we have to deal with each brother separately, we won't be able to dekulakize them because we won't have any grounds...And it'll be our heads that'll roll for failure to carry out instructions...'

'At this point Semka the Hedgehog interrupted:

'I'm warning you, Comrade Ikovians, anyone voting against this motion will be voting against Soviet power, against the Party. Dissenters could well follow them (he waved the exile list in the air) into the back of beyond. Just bear that in mind!'

'And so, I repeat,' continued the district representative, 'Who is in favour of dekulakizing Malkov, Mikhail Ustinovich and his sons Kirill and Ivan, expelling them from the village to sites stipulated by Soviet and Party agencies...

'Anyone against? No one. Motion passed *nem con!*'

So those two fellows who had burst into our house with the shotguns were under orders; one had a double-barrelled shotgun, the other had a single-bore hunting gun. Having shoved my brother along the bench, they sat down at the table and straightaway demanded to see my father's documents. He went into the next room and brought out the documents that all peasant farmers had to carry at the time. When they had ensured that it really was Malkov, Mikhail Ustinovich (father of his brothers), they served him with the summons, saying,

'Read it and sign.'

One may assume that the piece of paper was nothing more than the minutes of the meeting (of traitors), our fellow villagers, our neighbours who had sentenced us to long torment, and our father to death. Father mechanically took the piece of paper and read it slowly, asking Alexander to bring him a pen and some ink; then he signed and handed it back to the intruders.

Although we saw it all with our own eyes, it was beyond us to understand what was going on or why our parents, particularly father, was reacting so oddly upon realising why armed men had burst in. Perhaps he remembered the advice of his learned brother Timofei the younger who had advised the brothers to quit the farm and run away. But neither he, nor his brothers, had ever dreamed that Soviet power which had given them land was capable of doing such a dirty trick. How could they?!

Once they had done their duty, the unwelcome guests showed no sign of leaving. They settled down on the bench as if intending to spend the entire night sitting there. They instructed my father that nobody was to leave. Throughout the night, we kids slept like logs, but our parents did not sleep a wink: it was the last night they were to spend in their own home, the house they had occupied for only four years.

Next day the men got up and ordered us to get dressed, letting us take a hasty breakfast before telling us to gather up only the bare necessities—the rest we had to leave behind. The eight of us were herded together in the kitchen and then led single file into the yard. As we stepped down from the porch, I noticed a whole crowd of people standing there, obviously waiting for us to leave the house. You can bet your life that these were the very same people who had voted to expel us from the village the previous night. Now they had got up early so as not to miss the sight of us being led out of our own house, and so as to break in and grab all they could, or even take possession of the entire house. After all, only recently I discovered that an order had been issued from on high that part of 'kulak' belongings were to be distributed among the poor. So here was the poor—loafers and idlers who had come to get fat at the expense of others.

What remained was largely what our sisters had put by for their dowry: they were teenagers, after all; and then there was what our parents had put by for their own funerals. They got nothing from us children, for the simple reason that we had nothing.

In the yard they had already let the cattle out of the shed—someone had commandeered the barn. As I passed through the gates into the village street, I took a final look at the house and gates on top of which someone had nailed a sign saying 'Boycott'. None of us kids had the faintest idea what the word meant. We were taken under convoy by the same men armed with hunting guns to another street where we found ourselves at a shack owned by the political activist Aganka Bibkova. She had been among the impatient watchers waiting to rush into our house and pilfer and filch what she could. The shack had a single room which served as kitchen, living room and bedroom—no more than fifteen square metres in all—this was to be home for the eight of us. Father was made responsible for any attempt to escape from this hovel.

We all sat down upon the wall bench and stared into each other's eyes without taking off our coats. Tears rolled down the cheeks of Mother and Father. It was cold in this new place: it had obviously not been heated for ages even though it was now December and snow lay on the ground. If we had run away, maybe we would not have had such a terrible burden to bear, our mother would not have had to suffer so much, and Dad might have lived longer, instead of dying at the early age of 50.

It was hard to imagine what awaited us. Certainly we did not entertain any hopes of salvation from our misery. What hope could there be when our family had been driven out of our own home built by our father's hands, all without any trial? We were now 'living' in Aganka Bibkova's hut, and *Pravda's* leading article on 11 January 1930 contained the call:

'Declare war on the kulak, war to the death; wipe him from the face of the earth!'

That is what awaited us! Soviet power had decided to 'wipe us all, mother, father and children, from the face of the earth'; yet we innocent village kids were only 7, 9, 12 and 15 years of age! And if you count the children of my father's brothers, now branded as his sons by the text of the sentence (!), it was an even more pathetic picture:

Kirill had three children of six, nine and twelve; Ivan also had three children—aged one, three and seven. Altogether ten children, from one to fifteen years of age.

Having had a rest and a cry and bit of peace, my father and older brother Alexander then went into the yard to look for firewood. Perhaps Aganka had made arrangements to spend the winter in her shack? Or was it that she knew full well that she would soon move into a 'kulak house' which always had stacks of firewood?

Some time later, the two men returned with an armful each of firewood; there had not been any laid ready, but they had come across some broken fencing and cut it up for firewood. They lit the stove and Mother began to look round our new surroundings.

We stayed in Aganka Bibkova's hovel up to March 1930. Even now I just cannot think how our parents managed to feed us: all that we had put by for the long winter had remained in our old house—at the mercy of the dregs of the village, those who would condemn us to utter destitution. Yet we managed to survive almost to spite them, though not all of us.

The Long Journey into the Unknown

One March day in 1930, we had a visit from the same two fellows with the hunting guns, those who had kicked us out of our home; they ordered us all to get dressed, tie our bare necessities into bundles and await further instructions. We did not have long to wait. We were led out of the hut and, under armed guard, we were taken single file to the village council. Carts harnessed to sledges were standing on the square outside the council; we kids were sat in one sledge, our parents and elder sisters were put into the others—with Uncle Kirill's and Uncle Vanya's families as well as ours. Other 'dekulakized' families were allocated to other sledges. Everyone was standing around awaiting the word to move off.

All of a sudden our attention was drawn to an approaching sledge; the horse drawing it seemed familiar; when the sledge drew near we, kids and grown ups, realized at once that it was our beloved mare 'Breeze'. And who should be sitting in the sledge? Why, none other than Semka the Hedgehog and our 'old friend' Aganka Bibkova, owner of the hovel we had just vacated.

'Farewell, Breeze, our beloved horse, we won't be seeing each other again!' I could not hold back the tears which tumbled down my cheeks. 'Oh, Breeze, if only you could speak and do as you wish, you would never agree to pull people who had so pitilessly ill-treated your friends and ruined our childhood!'

'Let's go,' came a curt cry from the sledge—and off we went on our long, hard journey into the unknown. For many including our father, it was to be the final journey. A last glance at our native village disappearing into the distance. Oh, my dear cherished village, how many long, hard years were to pass before I would see you again! Yet it would be difficult to recognize you, fly-blown and god-forsaken, as the village we once knew as Ik. But for now we snotty-nosed village gutter-snipes, the youngest of whom was only seven, had fallen foul of Soviet power; it was trying to wipe us from the face of the earth as children of 'enemies of the people'.

We arrived that same day at the district centre, the hamlet of Yurgamyshch, which was no more than a railway station between Kurgan and Chelyabinsk. We were all bundled into a large hall like a concert auditorium. It was already bursting at the seams with families like ours brought from other villages.

It was so crowded you could hardly move: the entire floor was taken up with bodies and chattels. We could see straightaway that a good half of those sitting or lying on the floor were children like us and even younger; many were mere babes in arms, including Uncle Vanya's son who was just one year old. There was a terrible din: little children crying, and their mothers with them, especially those with tiny children, and grown ups kicking up a great hullabaloo. We could not find a place to sit down, so we had to spend the whole night standing up, pressed against the wall; all we succeeded in doing was to make a small place for our mother and little brother Fyodor; and that meant pushing and shoving to clear a small space.

At the end of the Civil War, and once the village had coped with the worst of the 1921 starvation, the countryside had begun to prosper after NEP's introduction. As scholars put it: war-ravaged farming was restored within three years. For the great bulk of peasant farmers, especially those 'who brought a horse home from market', reasonably good times were beginning. The only peasants not to benefit were those who 'brought only a concertina back from market'. The sad thing was that it was these so-called poor peasants who were to establish the collective farms. Village prosperity was helped by family growth: most families had between seven and ten children. Yet it was these relatively well-off large farming families that fell victim to dekulakization.

On the following day the hubbub and crying grew to fever pitch once more as we were led out to the station where a special train was waiting; it consisted of what we villagers called 'cattle trucks'. These trucks had been specially prepared for us: they had no bunks to lie on. You climbed through wide rough-hewn wooden doors, like farmyard gates, and found yourself in one big wagon with planks in each corner for one family. Since the number of families and bundles exceeded the wagon's space, you can imagine how overcrowded it was.

As the train moved off one of our relatives or perhaps it was merely a former neighbour who had not been at the meeting tried to bid us farewell, but the police and some civilians barred the way, stopping us from saying a last goodbye. I noticed a woman managing to shove Uncle Vanya's concertina into the wagon; he had played it at all our parties, especially in his youth on the village dance square. She evidently hoped we would find moments to sing to the concertina.

The terrible trouble with travelling in that cattle truck was that the timber walls let in the wind through all the chinks; so the wind simply howled about the truck. You had no protection from it without warm clothing; and we were not allowed to take any with us; it was 'surplus to requirements'. We had to sleep virtually on bare boards, buffeted about whenever the train sharply braked or went over bumps. Grown ups could bear it somehow, but imagine what it was like for women with children at their breast; they were like brood hens spreading their wings and pressing their infants to their breasts, warming them with their body heat, covering themselves and their child with some old bit of flannel blanket.

The 'Bourgeoika' stove in the truck emitted little heat, and what it did went straight out through the cracks; but we were able to boil or heat up some food for the mass of little mouths that had to be fed. Whenever the train stopped, we had to scrabble for coal or firewood ourselves because people had been warned in advance not to help the 'kulak' train in any circumstances. It was in those inhuman conditions that we journeyed into the unknown.

At one of the halts, the men were rounded up, handed saws and axes, and told that the train could go no farther owing to lack of fuel. Whether they liked it or not, the men had to fetch fuel for the engine if we were not to freeze to death in the Siberian wastes.

One early March morning in 1930 we were approaching a halt somewhere in the wilderness; we had noticed a large number of carts lined up alongside the rails; some of the adults guessed at once that they were for us. And, right enough, we were ordered out of the wagon and into the carts; now we continued our journey by horse-drawn cart.

Within the hour we had come to a village where the carts drew up and we were ordered to dismount. We were all billeted on the local inhabitants. As we were being driven through this village of Alekseevsk we could see that the houses and other buildings were fairly solidly built. For a few nights we lived with a widow and her adult feeble-minded daughter. Then we were transferred to another landlady whose house was bigger than our old home. Its yard was entirely covered with planed planks, and all along the side stood sheds, barns, lean-tos and a bath-house. We were put in one of the barns. The house itself stood on the high bank of the River Negla which flowed into the Sosva. Negla's floodlands stretched as much as a kilometre across. By the time we arrived, the entire surface had been covered with special timber rafts designed for floating down the river. The village of Koshchai stood on the opposite bank of the floodlands and that was where the administrative buildings were located: the village council, stores, school, club and church.

One interesting feature of Alekseevsk was that almost all its adult inhabitants were hunters. I was witness to their hunting festival: they tossed up bottles and shot them out of the air. The whole village had the same surname—Voroshilov. Our landlord was both hunter and carrier, delivering commodities from base to all the stores around.

Exile

Our major concern in the new setting was how we were to live. Our childhood evaporated as swiftly as smoke in the sky.

It did not enter the heads of our younger brothers Grigoriy and Fyodor that we had to find food somewhere or other; but I and my elder brother Alexander soon realized, as did the grown ups, that we had to do something to pay our way. My father was allocated work in the stables, while our two elder sisters and Alexander had jobs in forestry. We began to think as adults and, first and foremost, what we could do to assist our elders in earning some food.

As I wandered about the village in search of a job, I discovered that some locals would go to a spot on the Sosva River to catch fish. So one day, without informing or taking advice from my parents, particularly my father, I made up my mind to go fishing. I was keen to discover how they managed to catch the fish so that I could learn the trade and be successful at it. When I got back, I told my father and older brother of the need to obtain a net and fish hook; if they could do that for me,

I might be able to find some fish from which our mother could make fish soup for us all. When the tackle was ready, I took Grigoriy along as my assistant and we went off to the Sosva to catch fish. Each blessed day we would return with our catch, which brought much happiness to our mother and even made her cry.

Even though we had been dumped deep in the north, here too spring brought its joys: it was late March-early April. The sun warmed up the land, the snow quickly melted on the ice, large areas of melting snow formed and our path to the fishing grounds was blocked. No longer could we provide fish provisions for the family.

Grigoriy and I found ourselves out of work. When the floods passed and the water level in the river had fallen, we recommenced our simple craft, this time with fishing lines. And we were joined by other 'special migrants', as the locals and the village elders took to calling us. We joined together in a fishing party and made for the upper reaches of the Negla; we would start out in the evenings so as to be ready to cast our lines at dawn. We caught pike with the help of hair loops. Our help to the family was very welcome. Soon after, the authorities distributed a small amount of food, mostly rye flour, to all dependents. Naturally, it somewhat lightened our food burden.

When the snow had melted in the forest, all the 'kulak' menfolk living in Alekseevsk were assembled and the person in charge of the 'kulaks' announced,

'All of you have to travel twenty versts[1] into the taiga from Alekseevsk and construct a hamlet on the banks of the melting stream there; that's where you will live. I should warn you that you must build the hamlet over the summer, since your families are only permitted to stay in the village till autumn 1930. Irrespective of whether the hamlet is built in time, you will be excluded from the village.'

The 'kulaks' had no option but to set off the very next day for the banks of some unknown melting stream; all they had to build with—saws, axes and so on—were piled on to a cart.

Almost the whole family made the journey; only Mother and my two younger brothers, Grigoriy and Fyodor, stayed behind.

---

[1]A *verst* (Russian: *versta*) is an old Russian unit of distance equivalent to 1.06 km.

I set off for the taiga too. Half way to the designated site, we made a halt at a barracks which had been put up long before we had come to the area. The man in charge told us we would be living in the barracks while we worked at the new hamlet; it was eight versts from our workplace. Before we went any farther, each family was allotted places in the barracks; our space was for six people, including Uncle Kirill and Uncle Vanya. That done, we continued our long trek.

On arriving at the site, the supervisor pointed to a thicket, saying,

'Cut down this wood and build yourselves houses out of it. We'll bring you horses in the days to come and you can arrange the log-hauling to the building site with their help. Make insulating material from moss and lichen which can be treated in the nearby marsh. Once you've felled trees, people will arrive to lay out the streets and tell you where to put the houses. What we must do straightaway is to arrange brick-making for the stoves. That's your task—off you go!'

Inside the barracks were plank beds set along the walls. On one side they were shorter because a brick stove with a wide iron plate on top stood in the corner by one wall. We could make our food on it as long as we had something to dry out our clothes with. Right down the centre of the barracks, from one end to the other, was a trestle table with long wooden benches upon either side. The principal 'feature' of the barrack was its enormous host of bed bugs; there was no escaping them. So these were to be the wretched conditions in which we were to live for half the summer of 1930, walking to work each day, eight kilometres there and back.

Bearing in mind the terms that the authorities had set the 'kulaks' we had to hurry to build the hamlet; otherwise, our families remaining in the village might well have to suffer the same fate as when we had been driven out of our native village, without any trial. They would certainly not think twice about chucking out children, mothers and the aged; and right at the start of the Urals winter too!

You can imagine the utterly desolate place on the banks of the melting stream, with impassable taiga all around. In the spring of 1930, the authorities had driven former farmers there, the very best farmers, sticking the label 'kulaks' on them. That's how it was. All those people, and there were so many of them, were anything but idlers: they loved their work and were among the best farmers and craftsmen. And now, precisely for that, they found themselves in this god-forsaken place.

This band of 'hardened criminals' contained many fine lumberjacks, carpenters, joiners, blacksmiths, stove-makers and other tradesmen. They took their axes and saws and went to do battle with the taiga, since that's what fate had willed. The trees began to thin, the logs were measured and cut. My elder brother Alexander and I worked shoulder to shoulder with our father and our uncles, and our elder sisters Anastasia and Galina; we cut down trees, lopped off branches and burned them on a fire. Others built trestles for sawing the logs into planks, or dug pits for the house foundations; we selected a spot for brickmaking for the stoves. Young women and girls pulled up moss and lichen, threading it on slender strips of birch tree torn up with their roots and carrying it on their backs to the construction site as insulating layers between the rows of timber.

Horses arrived for the 'kulaks' to use for hauling logs to the building site; it was a good job they were handy at working with horses. None of the labourers had to be urged on or taught what to do in building houses: they knew their job better than anyone. Houses began to spring up like mushrooms after the rain; I don't know if the hamlet had any blueprint, yet streets took shape before my eyes; they were made up of identical houses of five by eight metres in dimension; for the moment they had just doors, two frames coupled along the centre of the opposite wall. Right in the middle opposite the window was a Russian stove, dividing the living space into two halves, each intended for a single family.

Once the horses had arrived, my brother Alexander and I had a new job: we would sit astride the horses harnessed to the front of a cart on which logs were piled, and we would haul them to the building site. This also enabled us to earn something for food and thereby help out our father and sisters.

In the spring of 1931 my parents pooled resources with our next-door neighbours to buy a cow. On our side, we paid for it with our elder sister's fur coat. I've no idea how she succeeded in bringing it to the hamlet. Anyway, once we had milk, our catering needs somewhat 'improved'. But soon after an unexpected disaster struck: one day our cow did not return with the rest of the herd. It took us three days searching through the forest to find her: our 'breadwinner' had fallen into a hole and died. We could not even use her meat.

An even greater misfortune overtook us in the summer of the same year: our father died. Someone said that he'd been kicked by a horse while working in the stables; this evidently brought on tuberculosis which eventually killed him. Yet the main cause of his death was different: since he was unable to support his children he just lost heart. It was this helplessness that really killed him. He could see our half-starved existence, he knew what was happening to his family, and his body just could not take it any longer. He died before my very eyes; I was standing beside his wooden bed, gazing at his face. Even as I write these lines, I can see him still. Yet I'm 77 now and he died when he was no more than 50. That's 'dekulakization' for you!

Just imagine what it was like to see your father die before your eyes, branded a 'kulak'. What had we children and illiterate mother done to deserve this fate? What crime had we committed against Soviet power that caused it to condemn us so?

We buried Dad in the taiga close by the house. It grieves me to think I've not managed to visit his grave, or even the cemetery where he lies buried. I've heard that the hamlet built by 'kulaks' and named Charakh after the nearby stream is now a prison zone, so you cannot go there anyway.

Our misery greatly increased with Dad's death. I do not have the words to describe the situation in which we found ourselves. The two grown-up sisters, Anastasia (deaf from birth) and Galina, realized that they could do nothing to help us, so decided to leave us and go off to live without any documents, while we stayed with our mother who was now over 50. They departed virtually with nothing, leaving us all the things they 'did not need', as they put it, so that we and Mother could take the bits and pieces to the neighbouring villages (some 40 to 50 versts away) and exchange them for provisions. But that was not so simple since anyone leaving the special migrant hamlet had to have the commandant's permission. And that was given only in exceptional circumstances which entirely depended on the whim of the commandant. All the villages of Sosva and Gagarin districts operated a ban on special migrants: they were not allowed to enter without the commandant's permission given on an ordinary sheet of white paper signed by him.

Therefore, in order to enter a village unhindered, I learned to imitate his signature and we passed unchallenged into all the villages. My success as forger came from having had four years of schooling before exile, and my handwriting was much better than many tenth-formers today. In those dim and distant 1920s our school had an unwritten rivalry among pupils for the best handwriting, and I invariable came out top. Since I had an original permit signed by Commandant Zaitsev, it was not hard to sign his name so well he would not notice the difference himself. At that time, there were not many people who could read and write in the villages, at any rate people who could tell a forgery from a genuine signature. Whenever we had something to exchange, I usually went round the villages with my mother. Sometimes, my brother and I would go alone. We used to enjoy going from house to house, begging and asking for charity. Folk gave what they could. And we managed to get by. We called it 'going about the world'. And when we had nothing to sell, Mother got work from some peasant farmers, putting by some grain 'for a rainy day'—if it was harvest time. We earned this from peasant farmers untouched by collectivization. It meant humping sizeable weights on our backs for some forty or fifty kilometres!

The grain we brought to the hamlet had to be turned into flour; for that purpose several families whose adult men were still alive possessed hand mills. We would turn to them for help. But we had to pay in grain for the use of the mills, and that diminished our stores and made our lives that much worse.

By the spring of 1932, all we had to exchange for provisions had run out and we had nothing to take to the villages. We now had to find some inner-hamlet sources, and these were quite paltry. After our father's death, my mother and I were considered dependents, so once a month we received a trifling amount of flour. It was from this flour and from what we managed to obtain ourselves that we survived; mind you, we could not dream of trying to bake a loaf of bread; that was a luxury we could not afford. We had to use the flour to augment the volume of what we dared to call 'bread'; our additives to the flour were dried and crushed swamp moss or dried and pounded lime leaves. Most of the time it was the other way round: we added a little flour for binding to dried and crushed moss and lime leaves. It was on this 'bread' that we nourished ourselves. Of course, there was always the great danger of stomach pains which could be serious enough to kill you, especially the elderly.

How relieved we were when the forest provided us with its bounty—mushrooms and berries. That improved our meals no end and enabled us to stock up for winter. But it was no use always trusting in nature's bounty; we had to do something ourselves.

At the end of 1931, we had an influx of 'kulaks' from the Ukraine, and they were housed in the spare buildings built by Russian 'kulaks'; among these newcomers was an old fellow who had been a blacksmith. I was assigned to him as apprentice. Not only did he bring his skills to the forge, he also brought many of his tools which he had been permitted to take with him when he was 'dekulakized'. He used to tell me all sorts of stories about his life as blacksmith.

His name was Belkin, Granddad Belkin. He was a good workman and I a good pupil. The old man and I became firm friends; he would always call me Vitya. I had nothing but the greatest respect for this remarkable man. Even now, as I write, I can vividly recall this short episode of my life at the forge, with the greatest of happiness; there I would be standing next to Granddad Belkin, my dear teacher.

Sadly, I did not have long to learn the trade from Granddad Belkin. He was already getting on in years; and more's the shame on those who so unjustly drove him into exile and broke him. He died soon after his arrival, though not before teaching me a great deal, even though I was then only sixteen. I would make all that the builders ordered from me at the forge: I forged nails, staples, various plates, heels, hooks and loops; I riveted ploughshares, made axes and did all the minor forging.

My wages were not a fortune, but they did enable me to help Mum out. Incidentally, wages were worked out only on paper: no special migrants were handed cash, they just had provisions allocated instead of wages. We did not even know how much we had earned and how many provisions, clothing and manufactured goods we had been allocated for our pains.

I had my seventeenth birthday in the autumn of 1933. In scrabbling to earn a crust of bread I had not noticed those five years passing since my twelfth birthday. I seemed never to have been a teenager. In those days we became adults straight from childhood, even though my height clearly marked me off from an adult; yet I had left my childhood far behind in my thinking.

Since 1929, by which time I had had four years' schooling, no further talk occurred about education. That was not because there simply was no school or even anything to write on or with. It was just that we were categorically banned from going to school in the nearby villages. In any case, our lives were such that there could be no thought of schooling, all efforts were bent on survival, not dying of hunger. It was only in 1933, when I was 17, that I and other kids were permitted to take up our schooling again in the neighbouring village. The age of the contingent of pupils was higher than that of normal school kids (13 to 15); it was closer to 20. One lad even had a black moustache.

Bearing in mind that children from many hamlets like ours were attending the school, the authorities arranged a modest hostel for us to stay at. The large room had a stove with cast-iron hotplate in the centre; it was here we cooked our humble fare, mainly potatoes. The school had its own dining hall which prepared a thin gruel once a day for us—from buckwheat or pearl barley; the gruel was doled out to pupils in dishes; mine was rather different from the normal plates—I used an ordinary empty can of beans which would be filled halfway.

Sverdlovsk and the Transport College

A recruiting officer from Sverdlovsk arrived at our school in the spring of 1936; he firmly advised us to sign up for further studies at the Sverdlovsk Transport College. To tell the truth, I had not given serious thought to entering this college or any other. But, I thought, if I'm invited to that college, I would learn to build roads—since we had none anyway. So I asked the officer to put me down as an applicant for the college; I was so keen to escape from the awful and humiliating environment of the special migrants, of which I was one myself! A lot of lads from our hamlet signed up; they included Aleksei Zhuravlyov with whom I attended the Charakh school.

We started to prepare our documents for the college; it was fairly simple since the special migrant office was at Sosva. We did the best we could, though we were very much afraid that, being special migrants, we would be turned down anyway. The fact that we got accepted is evidently due in no small part to the fact that the college came under the auspices of the Internal Affairs Ministry. So, there I was, for the first time in my life, at the age of twenty, receiving a certificate that recognized me as a human being—instead of possessor of a temporary, one-year passport.

When the time came to go to Sverdlovsk to take the entry examinations, almost all the Charakh youngsters assembled to travel the thirty kilometres from Sosva; it was more fun to go in a big bunch. In all my nineteen years I had only once, in 1926, gone to a big town—that was with my Uncle Timofei the Elder, from Sychevo to Kurgan, which seemed like a big village to me. Besides my village of Ik and the nearby villages I had never seen anything else. It was the same in exile: I had only set eyes on my own hamlet and the villages I'd visited to exchange goods. And now I was heading for the great city of Sverdlovsk. Just to think of it set my pulses racing, gave me hope for the future.

My thoughts were all centred on passing those exams since they would decide my entire future. So off we went on the same train from Sosva that had brought us here in the spring of 1930.

From the very first moment of arriving in Sverdlovsk, no matter where I looked, everything was extraordinary. On the way to the college I could not stop staring around me at such incredible sights. We had been assigned to lodgings in the college hostel for the duration of the exams.

I passed, and I became a student at the Sverdlovsk Mechanical Transport College. I relished the work. I was over the moon: before the host of fellow students I was no longer a special migrant, though I never forget that unique label; I was now one of the them, with equal rights. I joined the trade union almost at the start of the academic year, and then I joined the Young Communist League. I did so for the purpose of entering the college and to distance myself even further from being a special migrant, to consolidate my equal rights. From the time I commenced my studies I had no one to rely on for money; all my hopes were pinned on gaining a student grant. So I set myself two targets: to study well so as to gain recognition and...to pay my way—i.e. to guarantee myself a grant for good work.

The clothes in which I attended classes had been made by my mother's own hands, though she had never pretended to be a seamstress; she had made them from a few old rags. By modern standards, it would be shameful to go around in them even in the village, let alone in the city; in any case they were summer clothing. But I had no choice since there was nothing else for me to wear. When the frosts set in, there was no thought of appearing out-of-doors in my threadbare hand-me-downs—and it was all of a kilometre to the college; so I had to remain in the hostel. So as not to fall behind in my studies, I had to work after the other students had got back from lectures to tell me what had gone on.

Seeing my helpless situation, the other students appealed on their own initiative to the union committee at the college to make me a gratuitous loan to purchase some winter clothing. I was therefore given money to buy myself a light overcoat with side pockets; and it was in that coat that I went off for army duty in 1939.

Naturally enough, virtually everyone in our group knew that we from Sosva were special migrants, yet nobody mentioned it, no matter what cropped up during our studies. All that marked us off was our age: we were about three or four years older than the students not in our category and who had gone straight through school. Those students were all 16 or 17, while I was past 20; the funny thing was that I was lower than average height, so in some ways I looked closer to a sixteen-year-old.

I had hoped to serve my two years in the army and then return to my studies. But fate decreed differently. I had to experience all the terrible horrors of the war, and I was not to return to Sverdlovsk until 1945. But I was one of the lucky ones: only six returned out of our student group of twenty youngsters.

Subsequently, I spent my entire life working in the city public services department. Although the Soviet régime dealt cruelly with my parents, I can honestly say that none of us children turned into thieves or bandits. We came through it all despite the deaths and privations, taking no revenge on those who had dealt so savagely with us. We have borne and still bear our destiny as it was dealt out to us.

ANNA R.

ANNA is the daughter of a kulak; she was born in 1916. She was therefore fourteen years old during dekulakization. I obtained her address from the Department for Rehabilitation of Repressed and Dekulakized Persons, and wrote her a letter requesting an interview. I received her consent a few days later. This is what she wrote:

'Unfortunately, my hearing isn't so good these days, but I'll be waiting for you on Wednesday around four o'clock, sitting by the door. Please knock loudly.'

That was in October 1993, in our Transurals autumn.

On the appointed day and hour I knocked at the door of her apartment. Anna lives on the ground floor of a five-storey block of flats in Kurgan town centre. She has a tiny one-room flat with all modern conveniences: gas, electricity, central heating and running water. Her belongings are very modest—basic table, chairs, a small television set, carpet and special multi-coloured matting woven on a special weaving frame. The matting strikes me as a traditional peasant household item, though rarely seen these days in town; it reminded me of my grandmother's house; in fact, Anna herself, a very slim, tidy elderly woman, was quite like my own grandmother.

The sight of my recorder made her feel ill at ease, but she gradually began to talk freely. She wept several times during the interview: the events surrounding her tragic life were evidently firmly etched on her memory.

After the interview, for a long time she refused to take any payment. But at long last she said, 'Oh, all right, since Yeltsin won't give us any compensation, the money can make up for it.'

No money can bring back her health or the lost years.

Anna's story

Childhood

My grandfather arrived in the Transurals from Central Russia in the late nineteenth century. He came with his brothers and sisters of his own volition. They were all keen workers, got married to local girls—and that's how our family started.

Grandfather had a big family and he put them all to work. He couldn't abide slackers: he never ate 'unearned' bread and never gave it to others. He even used work as a panacea for all ills. Whenever he felt unwell he used to go out and chop wood!

Our family lived in the village of Tikhonovka, in Kurgan Region. It was a tiny place, with only forty households, yet a pretty spot. We had a stream running past where we all used to swim and catch fish in summer. As for the forest it was full of mushrooms and berries which we used to pick and put by for winter so as to keep ourselves alive through the long winter months.

I was born in 1916 and remember our village having only three well-to-do households; most of us were medium peasant farmers, with a smattering of poor peasants. My parents came from a long line of peasant farmers. There were eight of us children; a ninth was born just before resettlement. We initially lived with Grandfather, but then built our own home, with everyone giving a hand. Our farm stock consisted of four cows and four horses. Mother had all of us to look after as well as the house; she had no time for anything else. Father did what peasant farmers do: he ploughed, sowed and made all our footwear. He even gave us lessons since the village had no school. Naturally, all the children assisted Father in reaping, ploughing and furrowing, as best we could. We also had our own farm tools: a plough, mower and threshing machine, but they were split between the four brothers who took it in turns to use them. Often we didn't come home to eat because our land was a tidy distance away. Although we didn't own much land, the nearby Tatars were selling theirs and father purchased it and ploughed it up. If he hadn't done so, we wouldn't have had enough to feed ourselves. We milled our own flour at the windmill: and we also baked our own bread. In fact, virtually all our food was home grown, so to speak: meat, milk, butter and vegetables.

We dressed very poorly; nothing was bought. Mother made us canvas skirts which we shared; the men had canvas trousers, and our sheets were of canvas too. We sewed our own blankets, matting and table cloths; nothing was purchased. For the bed we had a piece of felt which Father would unfurl each night and we would all lie down upon it, in a row. Our house was quite large. Father had only just built it and not yet divided it into kitchen and living rooms. He didn't have time. Outside we had a barn, stable and several sheds. Our father made them all himself, with help from us.

I cannot say that religion passed us by. Dad was not particularly god-fearing, but he went along with religion since his mother and father were elderly and he respected his father's faith. The village had no church, so we had to travel ten kilometres to go to church in the next village. Mostly, we just didn't have the time and went only for Easter, Epiphany and Shrovetide, for the major festivals. Not that we neglected religion altogether. We had no Old Believers; we were all Russian Orthodox.

Our dekulakization started in 1928. It all happened surreptitiously. Our parents kept mum in front of us, so we knew nothing about it. I just started to notice people disappearing: first one, then another, and another. Exiles took place at night so that nobody would see. I only ever saw one family being carted off; I recall the waggon being full of children. All the rest simply vanished into thin air.

Then some villagers began to set up a commune; it attracted all the poorest and the laziest characters. Though we had no thieves and vagabonds in the village, we did have plenty of idlers. When a person loafs about, he earns nothing and starts to envy others who do. That's why the poor of the village became communist activists. They were in their element, cutting off their beards and plaits, even lopping off the horses' tails, shouting and bawling,

'We are Communards. Down with the kulaks!'

Meanwhile, the people who had to give up their cattle and poultry to the commune just sat and wept. My parents didn't join the commune, remaining single farmers—for which they were to pay dearly.

First they had a massive tax to pay; it was so high they were quite unable to pay it. They just didn't have the grain. After that, activists from the commune descended on us, breaking all the locks on the barns and clearing us out of all our corn. Next time they came to list our property. They noted it all down and carried it off, although there was really nothing left to take. Our furniture was all home-made; father had made all the tables, chairs and bed out of wood himself. It was all confiscated, along with the samovar, clothing and pillows. Incidentally, I later came upon one of those activists at the cemetery; she was begging for charity. Clearly she hadn't made good at others' expense and had remained as poor as when she had started out.

We were woken up in the night in early spring, 1929; we were told, 'You're going for good.' We didn't even protest, there was no point, since they were ignoramuses scared stiff of the authorities. They didn't even have any guns. It was two Young Communist girls from the commune and some activist or other from town. They knew we had nowhere to run to. How could Dad desert his family? And where would we kids go? Since they knew we wouldn't try to escape they weren't frightened of us. At dawn they lined several families up in the Rural Council building and then sent us off into the unknown.

Exile

First we were taken to some freezing cold barracks; I don't even know where they were. All I know is that we froze and starved a full ten days in those barracks. And then off we went farther in carts to Perm Region. Once there, all able-bodied men were rounded up and sent on foot to a logging camp. They were not even permitted to spend the night with us. We had no idea where they were being taken or for how long. They could even have been shot as far as we knew. We lost Father and our eldest brother who was then 20. Only later did we hear whispers that they were 25 kilometres from our settlement, cutting timber, but they were not allowed to visit us.

Women and children, meanwhile, were billeted in tumble-down shacks that were standing empty. Two families shared one such hovel, commiserating with each other. Mother fell ill straightaway, leaving me as the eldest to take charge. I had to look after my eleven-year-old brother and two younger sisters—but the sisters both died of hunger and disease in the first few months. My elder sisters had remained behind in the village since they had married poor peasants, which had saved their lives.

We knew terrible hunger in that settlement. I saw people drop dead on the street, without a bite to eat for ten days. All we got later was half a loaf of bread to last two weeks; we never set eyes on a whole loaf. Mother would divide our share into five pieces: we would eat for five days and starve for ten. Mother could hardly move from lack of food, my brother could not talk at all, he just lay there. As for me, I too suffered terribly, but I was determined to save them. I went into the forest for mushrooms which we boiled up in a pot and ate. When May arrived, they forced us to dig the soil and gave us chunks of bread for our work. The trouble was that I was the worst worker owing to ill health and my youth; the women were stronger than me and hard workers.

I would work in the daytime and go mushrooming straight after work. That's how we survived the summer. That autumn, father was brought back to us; but he was dying. They had brought him to that state after six months logging. He was only 43 years old. We learned from him that our elder brother had escaped; he wandered around for a long time, documentless, hiding here and there, before finally settling in Kurgan. It was three years before we were to meet up again. Father died that same autumn. He was conscious until the very last day, and he would tell us he could see Death approaching. First she was standing in the doorway, then she entered the room and approached his bed. Soon after, he told us, 'Not long now.' What with my brother lying there and Mother barely able to walk, there was nothing I could do to save him, even had I been able.

We gave Father a good send-off. We got hold of a coffin, dug a grave and even called a priest—a mighty rare event at that time. We gave him a fine funeral for a long-suffering peasant.

After Father's burial, the woman who shared the house began to nag at Mother about me going to work at the logging camp, to earn some cash; otherwise we'd all perish. I had no idea where the camp was, but was quite prepared to go and find it. Just as I was leaving, my little brother suddenly got up from his bed and started after me. God knows where he found the energy.

Neither of us had any shoes, so we went barefoot and my brother almost immediately cut his foot; it bled so badly, yet there was nothing to bandage it with. I would have taken him back had he not kept hobbling after me. It's here my memory fails me from the sheer misery of it all. I see it all as if through a thick fog. We must have walked about twenty kilometres before we stumbled upon some village or other. There we were given a bun and some money. Again I cannot remember the journey back; I do recall us not touching the bun, we wanted to keep it for Mother. When at last we reached home, all the neighbours came out to gaze at our prize. It was then that the woman we shared the hovel with began to pester Mother again.

'Take them away from here while you've still life in you. If you die, they'll die with you. You have some bread and some money, so go. When your money runs out you can beg.'

So Mother took her advice. Although it was a dreadful time, it was clear a mile off that we were frail, tattered exiles, which helped us get by. For the authorities never thought we were capable of escaping even if we had left the settlement. There was a boat station not far away, and we managed to get there by horse. While my brother and I hid in a corner of the boat house, Mother went to buy a ticket for herself on the ferry; she was so afraid she would not have enough money. But as luck would have it she had just enough to get to Kurgan. All of us kept well out of the way until the last moment, for fear of being sent back. But we made it, scrambled on board the ship and spent about two days on the river. When we arrived, we walked from the town to our native village. By now virtually nothing could have frightened us: winter was upon us and we were likely to die anyway, either from hunger or from the communists. At least we would be buried in our native soil.

Return to the Village

What did frighten us was being arrested again in the village; yet nobody touched us. Of course, we certainly must have looked pretty awful: a sick woman with her two emaciated children. We were given something to eat in the very first house we came to and told to go to the rural council for permission to join the collective farm. Mother was not accepted into the kolkhoz, however, but at least we were not expelled from the village. A kind-hearted woman, a widow with two young children, took us in and let the three of us live with the three of them. Once a week Mother would 'go out into the world' to ask for alms and I went to work as nanny with another family. Although I got no money for it I did receive food and some clothing.

Several times I went to the rural council to try to join the kolkhoz, explaining that there was no one else to feed my mother and young brother; I was head of the family. At long last, in 1931, I was accepted; I was fifteen at the time. By day I would do odd jobs about the farm, and of an evening I would attend school. It took me two years to get to form seven; the schoolmistress suggested I try to get into the Kurgan teacher training college: 'You're an able lass,' she said, 'but your health is poor, you shouldn't be working on the farm.' So off I went to Kurgan. In the meantime, my younger brother was completing a tractor course and was driving tractors on the collective farm. So I was fully able to leave Mother in his care. I arrived in Kurgan in the autumn of 1933; at that time my elder brother Pyotr was living in the town, the one who had escaped from exile. He had finally got his documents, thought they put him down as 'son of a kulak'. That is why he found it hard to find work; at long last he found a job as a stoker and held it until the outbreak of war.

I was so pleased to find him; we feared he'd met his death somewhere. While I was a student I often used to meet him in town. But in 1937 I gained my teaching diploma for primary schools and was assigned a school in the village of Vargashi. I loved the work and the children, and I got on very well with them. Unfortunately, I was only able to work there three years before I went down with severe stomach pains. The doctors said it was the effects of hunger and exile. I was diagnosed as having a stomach ulcer. So I waited until I was well enough to go home to Mother in our village. Once I arrived I began to seek work, since I was keen to stay home. By then it was getting on for June 1941 and war broke out. A lot of men were being recruited for war, so I was offered a job as secretary at the rural council. I had to deal with all manner of people coming with their problems, bosses telephoning from town, all sorts of orders. It all had to be recorded and conveyed to the rural chairman who then had to take decisions.

Hunger also came to the kolkhoz during the war. Every bit of grain they had harvested had to be handed over to the state; so all they had to eat was goose-foot grass and rotten potatoes, yet they worked up to fourteen hours a day. In wartime Mother and I lived in the same widow's house. There were six of us, all starving, yet never complaining. We would often sing songs and have fun to keep up our spirits. My brothers, first the elder, then the younger, went off to fight; and both were killed in 1943. So we never did manage to live a normal life together as a family.

Just Mother and I were left. We moved house several times during the war, taking over deserted homes; but when the owners returned, we again had to find somewhere else to park ourselves. At last we came upon a very kind woman in the village who told Mother she would lend her enough to buy a small house and a cow. She said we could pay her back later. She took pity on us, traipsing from one place to another. Mother hesitated about taking the money, afraid she would be unable to repay her; but I persuaded her to accept the kind offer. So we bought a house and a cow and life became slightly easier. The only pity is that Mother did not have long to live in her new house: she died in 1944. I buried her in the village cemetery and still visit her grave to this day. Sadly, I've never managed to get to Dad's grave; I'm just not strong enough. If only my brothers had lived.

The move to town

So I was now alone. I left the rural council since I found the work too finicky, it wasn't my cup of tea. I fixed myself up in the library and worked there fourteen years. I got married in 1947 and had a son, but my husband soon turned his back on us and we were divorced. I remained in the village until 1959. At that time, the local field nurse kept on at me to go to town for an operation on my stomach; I had put up with the pain getting on for twenty years. The problem was that you couldn't take up residence in the town without permission; so I got a temporary permit to stay with my cousin. I actually found myself a room in an apartment, although the landlady didn't allow my son in. I finally persuaded a woman to take us both until the New Year, when I intended to send my son to his father in the countryside. But my son was so distraught that he went to the landlady and begged her to let him stay. You can imagine his joy when she finally relented.

I had a stomach operation in early 1960. I had asked the doctors to do what they could without an operation; surely they had some medicine to help me? I had got by without surgery for twenty years. But they were adamant: my stomach was in a bad way, with one ulcer on top of another. The operation was unavoidable. I stayed in hospital for nigh on six months; they removed a good two thirds of my stomach, leaving just the upper part. As a result, I qualified for a Group II disability pension and was excused work.

While I was in hospital, my son was put in an orphanage before going to study at engineering college. Initially he was a full-time day student, but my pension didn't extend to two people; so he switched to evening classes, working by day and studying of an evening. Once he completed his course, I tried to persuade him to go on to university; I was so keen for him to get the best out of education so that he could stand on his own two feet. I would have scrubbed floors to enable him to study further. I succeeded in persuading him and he entered university, gained a place in a hostel. Content, I decided to return to the village. I still had my house there, the one Mother had bought. When I arrived at the farm, I found other people living in my house and they refused to let me in. But I was determined to fight it through the courts, while I rented a flat. I had no money to pay a lawyer, which was why my application lay unattended for a good six months in the court. At last, a lawyer agreed to take up my case free of charge. I told him I was disabled and responsible for keeping my son. Thanks to that lawyer I got my home back, though it took a month for the squatters to move out.

I spent nearly a year there before deciding to move back to town to be near my son. I was finding life hard in the countryside, and he was having a tough time in the hostel. He was sharing a tiny room with four others, having to clean and cook for himself. So in 1966 I sold my house in the country and bought a small cottage in town. By then my son had to leave for national service, and after that he got married and completed his engineering degree at night school with his wife.

Our house was pulled down in 1970 and we were given two well-appointed apartments, one for me, the other for my son and his wife. We could have had a single three-roomed apartment, but I didn't get on with my daughter-in-law, so I thought it best to live alone.

That is how I live today. I survive on my pension, though there is never enough to eat. My son visits me once a week. I tell him to call just in case something happens; I don't want my corpse lying around. He doesn't stop long. All the same he helps out when necessary. And when I spent eight months in three different hospitals in 1986, I would not have survived without his help. He supported me all through my severe illness. He would come to visit me in hospital twice a week, bringing me something hot to eat. The food was so disgusting in the hospital, with special food for my dodgy tummy. He still brings me something to eat, though I won't take any money from him; I make do on my pension. I don't need very much, living alone.

My grandson was born in 1971. When he left school he followed in his father's footsteps, taking a job as a laboratory assistant in an institute and studying at evening class. He got married last year and is combining work and study, like his wife. They never come to see me; I suppose an old lady is not much fun. But I don't mind too much, as long as they are happy.

Battle for Rehabilitation

I heard about rehabilitation from the newspaper *Argumenty i fakty.* The article said that victims would receive various benefits. At that time I needed some dental treatment and had to wait ages before my turn came. I was hoping that I would avoid the long wait with my rehabilitation certificate. So off I went to agitate. My agitation lasted a full eighteen months. Initially I handed in my application to the rural council where we had all been resettled; but they didn't accept it, saying that no one could help me. Then I took my application to the police regional department; they started to interrogate me. No evidence remained in the regional archives. Can you imagine? People were being despatched to the Far North every day, to their deaths, and no records remained. So then I took it upon myself to compose lists from memory of all our village exiles; I totted up some eighty people. This time the police sent my application to Perm Region, Chelyabinsk Region and even to the Moscow Rehabilitation Centre.

I went with a lawyer and said,

'How can it be? Living witnesses to our exile exist, and yet I cannot do anything about it—explain!'

They advised me to apply to the regional court. From there my application once more went back to the rural court. It got ferried about all over the place, back and forth, back and forth. And I had to follow it from one place to another. They couldn't help me anywhere. At last I decided to appeal to local deputies who sent my application to the chairman of the regional court with a demand that he sort things out. Finally, they appointed a day for the hearing on 23 February 1993 and invited three witnesses. I named three people and sent the information to the court. Even then the first hearing never took place owing to a flu epidemic; only one woman turned up. As soon as my witnesses were well again a new hearing date was set. And everyone appeared in court: an old man from our village, a former pupil any my neighbour.

The court was in session. Each was called up in turn and questioned. They all told it as it had happened; they could hardly make up a story like that!

The court's verdict was to rehabilitate our whole family. It still took me a long while to obtain the certificate, but when I did I passed it on to the pension department. I didn't even keep a copy for myself. Well, I did get a bit more on my pension for repression and war. But I never saw any benefits and I'm still awaiting a law on compensation to the victims of collectivization.

As long as Yeltsin has not signed the law, I'm not going to tell anyone I was dekulakized, otherwise people will think I was some sort of landowner or landowner's daughter. Before perestroika I had not even told my son; he only learned of it recently. I don't think we ever were kulaks, just exiles. We never had any wealth and we suffered for nothing. I think Stalin must have had a dizzy spell, that's all.

YEVDOKIA G.

I CAME to hear of Yevdokia G. through one of my students. I was giving a lecture on 'Social Genealogy' and asked students to raise their hands if any of their family had been dekulakized; in each of my five seminar groups as many as four to six people put up their hands. Unfortunately, not all their grandparents were still alive; life in Russia is not conducive to long life, but some elderly people have inherited such a good genetic constitution that they have survived in spite of life-destroying Soviet policies. When one student told me all about her grandmother, I felt that this was the most promising, and I sought permission for an interview. This took place in May 1993.

Yevdokia G. lives in the village of Ikovka, about fifty kilometres from Kurgan. At one time her house resounded to the babble of children's voices, yet nowadays it is uncommonly quiet by contrast with the city hubbub; it's as if life here stood still a score or more years back. An old wooden cottage, old furniture, old woman.

Yet during the interview I sensed the remarkable zest for life this woman possessed. Just one tenth of the sufferings she had experienced would have been enough to bring down any one of us. And yet here she was at 72, working away in her garden and supplying her two sons in town with vegetables and fruit. In summertime they bring their families to see her and the house really comes to life. In winter, however, she is left alone with her memories; and what memories they are...

Yevdokia's story

I was born in 1921 in the village of Nikolskoe, Chelyabinsk Region. It was a small village with about eighty houses, split down the middle by a stream, an extremely pretty little stream. We would all swim in our own river when summer came and have lots of fun. Our forest was a real treasure house: we'd go there for grass and herbs, and for birch juice, and we'd play games in and out of the trees. It really was a merry old village with good solid houses, both of wood and of brick, though no more than four were brick built. We even had a little village store run by a local woman.

My parents were middle peasant farmers. My father, Vladimyan, could read and write, though I've no idea where he went to school. Mother, though, was barely literate. My father's first wife had died, leaving him a couple of kids, Taisya and Ivan. Then he married our mother and had another four children; there were two more, twins, but they died in infancy. Our household had three horses, four cows, some sheep, and bees too.

Dad did not involve himself in the farm; being educated he had a job as council chairman in the next village. Then he became manager of a butter works; in other words, he neither worked, nor lived with us at home.

Someone had to do the chores, though; and while the kiddies were still little we always had a woman to help out and some labourers. Then Ivan, the first wife's son, caught TB and died, he must have been about twenty, I guess. I remember him well. Grandfather and Grandmother lived with us. Grandma died before collectivization began, and Granddad died in 1933.

So I had three sisters, four if you count the one from the first wife, Taisya. Well, they gave a hand with the farm chores. I recall us keeping pigs and looking after the beehives; it was the usual sort of farmstead. Our neighbours were decent folk; the man's name was Andrei; they had seventeen children. Of the seventeen only one survived, the rest died. Eventually they went off to the goldfields, that's where their last daughter died, so they remained childless. My mother went to the funeral, that's the sort of good neighbours we were.

On our other side we had neighbours who were fairly badly off, though they did have a small farm. How did they live, you ask? Well, they had a roof over their heads, four sons, all the farm roofs were of wood, they had some sturdy horses, he was the blacksmith and all the time I knew him he'd be walking about in a grubby apron. But then he got resettled, God knows what for. Maybe because he worked at the forge and saw everything. What was there worth seeing, though? Once they'd resettled him, the whole household was broken up. Then others began to be evicted. This was in 1929.

Our father was a wily old bird. When he saw the way the wind was blowing he went into hiding, so they wouldn't touch us. He left us five with Mother and his old parents. At the time everyone was being signed up for the collective farm, they'd keep you up all night to get you into the kolkhoz. The trouble was all the commune members were poor and hadn't a bean. But it was us they needed, we had everything: all the machinery and horses and cows. No consent was sought, it was all done by force. They ordered Mother to go to the village council, kept her there all night and forced her into it.

Stories went the rounds that once you signed up for the commune everything would be shared, even your underwear. Our grandmother, now, had tons of jumpers and skirts, she was short and stocky, our old grandmother, and she put them all on and just sat there waiting. When our neighbour asked her why she was all dressed up, she said that if the commune wanted her clothes, they'd have to rip them off her back.

The commune boss was a poor peasant, Katya. She had four sons, a tiny cottage, as poor as a church mouse; she hadn't a penny to her name. Yet all of a sudden she started sporting some fancy fur coat, being commune boss and went round evicted homes throwing her weight about.

The victims were packed off to Chelyabinsk Region, five families at one go. One house became the kolkhoz office, another Katya's new home. Just down the road from us was a nice house; they turned it into a chicken run. And this Katya comes round, chucking us out, making us follow her to an empty hovel; and we'd beg her, 'put us down for something, Katerina.' True, when winter came and the barn was freezing cold, she did assign us everything that was frozen. We had to eat something. After all, people were being evicted and we had to get by somehow. Well, Mother was always on at us not to run riot in the village, not to pay attention to what was happening, not to profit at others' expense. Yet others, they used to grab everything they could get their hands on, they'd just come and snaffle it up. Not that there was much to take: maybe a rickety table and bunk, perhaps sheepskin coats and furs put by in the chest. They'd filch all the grub in the barns: grain, meat, cows. The whole lot would go, leaving the place bare. They'd sweep up every last grain of wheat, drag off the cows, drag off the horses.

They mostly kicked out those who had lots of kids. Then they'd bundle them into a cart, and there'd be no room for any belongings. All the poor wretches could carry were little cases for a change of clothes, abandoning their cows, horses and so on. The Vasilievs kept bees too, but why were they chucked out? He had five or six little kiddies, Olga was my best friend. So many children they had to build a new house; and that was their downfall. Father, Mother, half a dozen children, and such good bees too, and they went and got evicted, that's all there was to it. Off the family went, and where to? To some flyblown place, Yemanzhelinsk in Chelyabinsk Region, they spent the winter living in tents, the whole winter. They all caught colds, some died.

We had no kulaks in the village, people got evicted for nothing. I can still see it now, I was nine at the time. I remember how sorry we felt for them. My elder sister Taisya was in love with some fellow and went off with him as well, yet she soon came running back when winter set in. She said it was dreadfully damp, back-breaking labour, nowhere to live.

Once Mother signed up, joined the commune, the communards came and confiscated all we had. They broke up the barn where we boiled the pigfood in a big vat, it held about thirty buckets of swill; it was attached to the pig shed, but the whole lot got smashed up, all four walls, broken up and carted off. They seemed to delight in seeing who could wreck most. That's what confiscation meant, taking your barn. We had a fairly big farm, by all accounts; it could have made a decent kolkhoz itself. As you went in, there'd be five mangers on the left and five to the right. We had an outflow, all the water would flow down it, all the sewage. So you see, we were pretty modern. The cows were tethered, we had troughs attached to the well for them to drink.

We had a stallion and, as far as I can recall, two or three horses. The stables were made of new timbers, but they got wrecked too. Not the poor folk, though, they'd nothing to smash up; still, officials made an inventory of their possessions. It was in their interests. We had all the machinery. They took our cows, took our horses and made a kolkhoz out of our farm, made a calf-house out of our barn, vandalized the whole lot. And another thing: we had a bee garden, and they confiscated all our bees as well; the bees became communards and Mother had to go and look after them.

And then about a month later they decided to evict Mother. One time she came and told us she was being chucked out next day. My little sister had no idea what that meant, she was only three. All night we cried and talked about it, then next day we were all bundled into a cart, all five of us next to Mother; I can't remember now who drove us all the way to Chasha. Once we arrived at the police headquarters, Mother was taken from us and we all wailed and screamed, all together; I was nine then, and there we were screaming our heads off. It didn't do any good. They chucked Mother out, took everything from us and sent us back: four kids and Granddad who only had one leg. Nothing to eat, nothing to drink, nothing to wear, they took every last item, even the sacks we'd taken with us.

They took whatever they fancied. Yet we were only little, I was only nine years old, and Granddad was blind and only had one leg; yet they took all we had. We didn't even have any clothes to go to school in. We had had everything, lived well, I'll never know why we were left in the village. All the same, I went off to school next day with my sister Tonya, she was eighteen months younger than me. The others were just tots, the youngest being Sima who was three, she was born in 1927. Lena was born in 1925. That's how little we were. And we took them on a sledge, Tonya and I, to a nursery or kindergarten, over the other side of the river, even though we were kids ourselves. There we all were, no one to look after us, starving. We'd go to the kolkhoz and they might give us a frozen beetroot or cabbage, that's all. We had had everything, now we were penniless, starving. All we could do was beg; my sister Tonya went round the houses, though I didn't, she took a tablecloth to sell or exchange for food, that's all we had between us and starvation; they'd taken our cow and all, there was nothing left. Even if no one wanted the tablecloth, they might spare a few coins for us kids, something to keep the wolf from the door. That's what we'd been reduced to.

Now we took in washing as well; Mother had done all our washing for us. We had to rinse it all in the stream. Remember, I was only nine, yet here I was washing, going down to the stream on the sledge and rinsing clothes in the freezing water, this was wintertime. My hands and feet were frozen stiff; there was no place to do the rinsing at home, it wasn't done. Why I can't say. Nobody had done it before. But the woman opposite, Katerina, comes over and says, 'Don't you go traipsing down to the stream, fetch some water from the well and give the stuff a good rinsing at home.' After that we drew water up out of the well and carried it home. Jesus, it was cold. But that's how we washed and scrubbed. And that's how we managed to get by.

Did I tell you they'd pinched all our firewood and logs as well? Not a sausage left. Well, we did have the old stables, pretty ancient they were, with roofing of poles and stakes. So that winter we clambered through the snow, up on to the roof and tossed down the roof poles for sawing. There was me and my sister, she was younger than me, and Granddad. What an old grumbler Granddad was! We weren't sawing properly, kept losing our felt boots in the snow—we only had one pair between the two of us, and Granddad was moaning and groaning that we weren't doing it right. But we managed to saw it up into logs, all the poles and stakes; then we set to breaking up the stable until we had enough wood to tide us over the winter. We chopped and sawed all by ourselves; we had no option since they'd taken all our wood, and then abandoned us. You'd think they might have put us in an orphanage, wouldn't you?

We didn't even have any buckets; they'd taken them too. We wrote to Mother, asking her to send us a bucket. If we'd have been older, we probably wouldn't have dared write to her. All we had left was an old pot, full of holes and made of cast iron, it was ever so heavy, we had to wash the floor with it, though we could barely lift it. They'd taken everything. Don't ask me why.

Mother's Return

We began to kick up a fuss about getting Mother back; you see, Granddad died in 1933. He died on May Day, as I recall, and we gave him a decent funeral. Thankfully we only had ten days without him before Mother arrived. But what a welcome awaited her: our garden had been unattended for three years, it was all overgrown. We'd tried to dig it up, though we'd nothing but our bare hands, we didn't have the strength. While we were working on the garden, Mother fell ill with typhus. She had to go to hospital. But how? The kolkhoz, summer, all the horses in use; we had a go all the same. Our old horse, the stallion, was now on fire duty, but we chased up Maxim, our old stable lad, he knew Mother and we went along with him to the chairman and got permission for him to borrow the horse. So he mounted her up and took her to hospital. She couldn't walk anyway. We'd tried to plant some vegetables, but she was too ill to eat anything. Not that our efforts had come to much: no potatoes at all, it meant waiting till next spring.

We had a bit of clothing left, so we went round the houses trying to swap it for some potatoes. Better to buy potatoes than dress up. That's how bad things were. Mother had gone off to hospital, which meant we had seven kilometres to walk, in bare feet (we didn't have any shoes or boots) to see her. Anyway, we got there somehow but she wasn't allowed out to see us. Typhus, she was delirious, in a fever. And then, one fine day we turned up at the hospital and she tells us they're letting her out. She came out to us by the hospital wall, and we had to prop her up. But how were we to get her home, seven kilometres? She sent us to the village of Vosyanovo where she had an uncle; he was a single farmer and might be able to help. So we walked the seven kilometres to Vosyanovo. We got there goodness knows how, since we'd never been there before. Anyway, we made it and found the uncle who said he had a horse, but nothing to harness it to. Well, off we went home again, ten kilometres this time, again on foot. When we arrived, we were frantic: what were we going to do? How would we bring Mother back? Off we went once more to Uncle Maxim, and then to the chairman, Mother had to be brought home, who would help? Our old horse was idle but there was no cart. Well, to cut a long story short, once more we got permission for Maxim to ride to hospital.

Mum made it back home and we stretchered her into the house on planks, she was just as sick as ever, but asked us, 'Girls, pick me up and take into the garden.' Mum being big and us small, she took hold of our shoulders and we did the best we could, staggering along with her, but all three of us tumbled over in a heap, bawling our heads off. It was no good, we couldn't carry her to the garden. But she was insistent: we had to try to pick her up again even though we didn't have the strength. But we managed it somehow and she was able to see a bit of green coming up while she'd been in hospital. After that she began to get well, and we were given a cow from the kolkhoz. You should have seen us trying to milk her: we had to chase her all round the yard before cornering her. In the end she produced a good litre of milk a day. Something had to be done with it; we couldn't allow ourselves to scoff it all on our own. So we made some sour cream and every Saturday or Sunday Tonya used to walk seven kilometres to Chasha to sell a glass of sour cream. It was the only money we had. That's how we got by.

The years '33 and '34 saw a lot of starvation everywhere. We had to go out and mow goose-foot grass, gather it up and pound it into meal to eat. Mother used to go to work, often unable to get home for the night; she'd be working all day long, then guarding the barns all night, then back binding stooks the next day; she'd get as many as twenty-five all bundled up, a fair old shock worker she was. All for sticks (one 'stick' equalled a labour day; instead of money they'd put a stick up for each day worked). What they gave us was hardly worth the effort. We'd be toiling on the farm all day long, every day, weeding the wheatfields, treading barefoot through the brambles and stinging nettles, we'd weed the potatoes; a good twenty of us working in a whole brigade. When we were a bit bigger, we used to do the raking and sweeping, though we were still too little to do any mowing.

There wasn't a crust to eat, we were always hungry. Mother used to give us what she could from the fields, carrying it in her apron—some oats or peas; when she left home she never knew whether she'd find us dead or alive on her return. I forgot to say that when Mother was out one day my little sister was taken away. Our father's new wife came—he'd got himself another wife—and took my little sister. So that's how things were. He later wrote us a letter saying he'd take me in as well.

In Search of Work

I could see how tough it was for Mother to feed us all by herself, so I decided to go to my father. I stayed with him until 1936, until I'd completed seven classes at school, and then someone informed on him and he landed in gaol. I didn't fancy going back to Mother, so I made up my mind to go down south to Kazakhstan where we had some relations.

I arrived. I had no money, not a penny, no shoes on my feet, I arrived virtually with what I was born in. And I got a hostile reception; the relatives were scared stiff of getting into trouble for taking me in. Where was I to go? I ended up scuttling off to another village, ten kilometres away, where we also had some relations. But they had such a big family that with me around it would have been even worse. So I went back to my father. Once there I heard the police were looking for me, so I went to another village to Dad's friends. When I got there, the fellow told me he knew of a local bigwig who was looking for a nanny: would I fancy the job? I said, fine, I'd give it a go; the woman came and looked me over and said, 'I'll give you ten roubles, come along, you'll live with us and look after the children.' I told her I had no shoes, nothing to wear, nothing to change into or anything. She says, 'I'll give you all that.' Fine, she was as good as her word: shoes, clothes, a change of clothing. I stayed with them a year. Then I fell sick and the younger sister came to take me away; she too was from the country; we left, she would try to fix me up with a job somewhere else. She was living in Kazakhstan at the time. Well, I ended up staying with her, but I couldn't get work at all, they were cutting down anyway at the time. So I returned home again, went back to Chelyabinsk.

Once I arrived in town I had to go round searching for relatives once more. My uncle was living there. But I discovered that he too had been picked up and kicked out of his home. All the same, I did find another relative, a distant one. He took me in on condition I paid my way. This time I went to a garment-making mill, got a job and was doing it for a month, yet couldn't get a ration book. They had their pockets stuffed with coupons, yet I was sitting and starving. Still, at home they couldn't let me starve to death under their roof, so they gave me any scraps and soup leavings. There was nowhere to go, I was starving and feeling pretty awful. In the next flat was a woman suffering from TB, and I used to look after her, do the washing, scrub the floors every day. Not that it helped me get my hands on a ration book. So I quit my job, I had no option. I just packed it in, but where to now? I went to work on an allotment. I hadn't been working there long when I got a dose of malaria; I was shaking all over. They carted me off to hospital where I just sat around, lying there and wondering what would become of me. I was so weak I couldn't stand up without toppling over. My cousin came to look after me and, little by little, my condition improved.

Next I went to my uncle who had just bought a house. I used to lie on top of his stove to keep warm until I had completely recovered my health. I'd come without a penny to my name, I'd sold all I had, scrimped and saved and lost it all, I was left with nothing. One day Uncle says to me, 'Come on, let's go and buy you something.' So I went out with him and his wife and they bought me some oranges; then I ran off to sell them, for three roubles each, not bad. That would help me get by. Next day the same; with the proceeds I'd buy myself a bun, the cheapest going. That's how I kept myself alive for two or three weeks. One day I bumped into an old friend who said I looked as brown as a gypsy, running about all day under the sun. I told her that gaining a crust to eat hardened me up; you had to keep your wits about you. 'Why don't you get a job nannying?' she asked. Where would I find a nanny's job? 'Come home with me,' she says, 'I'll pay you thirty roubles and give you your keep.' Right. They had a sick son, TB of the groin; so I would be tending him. I stayed a year with them. She sewed, was a seamstress; but the police got on to her and refused me residence. I was on my way again. But she says, 'Not so fast, don't cry over spilt milk, you just stay until you find somewhere else, stay as long as you like.' Anyway, it wasn't long before someone heard of my plight. We had a visit from the wife of the garment factory manager. And my mistress gave me good references. This was all while I was out, I'd gone to market for some bread. When I got back, my mistress told me all about the visitor and how she wanted me for this and that, was offering twenty roubles.

Since I had nowhere else to go, I went to this family and stayed three years with them. In the course of time they got me into a nursing course. The woman put it this way, 'Listen, my dear, you've no one to support you, should you fall sick tomorrow you'll be no use to me. So I'm arranging for you to study to be a nurse, OK?' I jumped at the chance. By day I worked for them, and by night I went to college. That lasted all of ten days, then she shook her head and said it wasn't working out. Maybe I'd like to switch to a shop-assistant's training course; I was as strong as an ox by now, I could cope with that. So she dressed me up, stuck a hat on my head, and put lipstick on me, I was done up to the nines.

They told me I wouldn't qualify for a student grant, only the army and navy stores gave grants, but I could study and train free of charge. I took it. I'd saved up about three hundred roubles, enough to live on; I'd manage somehow, try to earn a bit on the side. Anyway my mistress promised to help me out. That went on for a couple of weeks, and then the principal told my mistress he'd fix me up as an apprentice. I was only a young slip of a thing, he said, and needed a bit of cash, he'd fix me up in good stores, selling kitchenware. So I went for an interview, got the job and things went well. I was earning forty roubles. It wasn't really enough to live on, and the others would help me out now and then, a rouble here, five roubles there. I got by. But then they started to lay staff off; they could hardly sack the senior staff, could they? I was in tears, but the manageress told me not to cry, she'd get me transferred to another shop, a foodstore. I said I had no experience of selling food, how would I manage? 'Never mind,' she says, 'you'll learn, soon get the hang of it.' Okay, off I went to the foodstore, go in and who should I meet but an old acquaintance, he'd been working there as a manager. So I say, 'I've been sent here, I'm nervous.' 'Don't you worry,' he says, 'I've been here two or three years, I'll show you the ropes.'

All looked set fair when I had the police on my track again, coming all the way from the country to inform everyone that I was 'dekulakized'. I had no choice but to quit my job. And once jobless I had no documents, no passport, no work book; I could only sit at home. A knock on the door, a bloke in civvies comes in and asks, 'Is so-and-so here?' 'That's me,' I say. 'Get your things, you're coming with me to the station.' He didn't say the word 'prison'. 'Bring some clothes and nothing else.'

Well, I gathered up my things, not that I had much to take. Where I was going there'd be little need for much anyway; I wasn't going anywhere. And there I was on my way to gaol. I was scared out of my wits, I'd never been to prison before. I began to lose blood, even had blood in my diarrhoea. What to do? I was thrown in a cell, I just sat there, lay down on my bunk, one day, two; then my legs just gave way and I couldn't get up. They put me in hospital. I was there a month until gradually movement returned to my legs. I wept and begged them, 'For Christ's sake, don't put me in a prison camp. I'm no criminal. I'll go back to the country, I've a mother and sisters there. Let me go, please.'

Well, they drove me to the station all right, but sent me with a lot of other convicts to a prison camp. We all piled into a wagon and I found myself with another runaway like myself; she told me her story and I felt better having some company. They took us to Kazakhstan. There they pointed out an office: go and tell them who you are. So the two of us went, the train chugged off and we were left alone. When we got to the office and told our story, we found the officials were at home asleep. 'Find yourselves some room on the floor,' we were told, 'and in the morning they'll be here to deal with you.'

When the foreman finally came, we told him our story, and he brought us some bread and fed us. We stayed there another night, on the floor again, while they were making out our documents, putting all the signatures on them and assigning us to the main office.

The foreman asked me who I was, where my relatives were, and I told him they were in the countryside; that's where Mother and my sisters lived, in Nikolskoe. 'Well, why don't you go and join them?' he said. I said I didn't have any money to travel anywhere. 'Nor do we,' he said. 'So we can't give you any money. Maybe you've got some relations here somewhere? We could arrange for you to stay with them.' 'No, no, I don't want to stay here; I want to go home to my mother.' I then heard that there was another woman wanting to go to her relatives in our village; if she could help me out with some money, I could leave too. Off I went to find the woman and talk her into helping me. Finally I arrived back in 1941.

War

No sooner had I got back than war broke out. Virtually all the men joined up and I went to work on the kolkhoz, since workhands were in short supply. At first we all wailed, even the dogs howled; but you can't weep forever, you had to get on with it. All the women went out into the fields. They used cows to plough, some used oxen—all the horses were commandeered for the front. We had to mow hay, bring in the harvest, sharing out the jobs. Shortly after, the 17-18 year old men were called up, leaving just the old, the women and children behind.

How we worked: from dawn to dusk; we'd be working every day in the fields until the snows came. We'd only come home on Saturdays, have a wash and a bit of sleep in our own home, our kolkhoz, under a single blanket, so to speak. My mum would be home, working away indoors and outdoors in the garden, while we would be slaving day and night in the fields.

They still wouldn't give us any passports in case we fled to town. I only got a passport when I married, after the war.

In wintertime we would peel potatoes, dry them out by the stove and hand them in. They were for the forces, that was the order. We knitted socks and sent them too, doing our bit for the war effort. We worked with a will, dead keen we were. When you look around today you don't see people like that; it makes me cry just to think of it. Folk work badly these days; there's only one gang that works well—the swindlers. Everyone tries to do you out of something and slip the proceeds into their pocket. In the old days, we'd share everything, give each other a hand, consult each other, never dream of stealing; there was no need for padlocks in those days. It was unthinkable; it's not the same any more. People seem crippled nowadays, no legs to stand on, they'd have a fit it they had to do what we did. It was a matter of life or death for us.

I worked about a year on the farm, and then heard that Chasha needed chemists. It was one way of escaping from the kolkhoz. I decided to try my luck. So I walked the ten kilometres to the district centre and got taken on. I wrote out prescriptions, made up various powders and creams. I liked the work so much that in 1942 I applied for medical college in Tomsk. At that time my father was living there with his family; he had just got out of prison. While studying at college for two years I stayed at my father's. We had three hours of study and three hours of training on the job. While at college I joined the Komsomol so as to get right away from the stigma of being a kulak's daughter; and when I graduated I was called up, as a Komsomol member. Luckily, the war was drawing to a close and I accompanied the troops through various lands: Romania, Bulgaria, Czechoslovakia, and I spent Victory Day in Dresden. We went straight to Moscow by train from there; we travelled so fast that we hardly had time to wash and take a drink at the stations. No sooner had we arrived in Moscow than we were told:

'The train's moving on, war has begun with Japan!'

That dampened our spirits, of course, we were so keen to get home. Then all of a sudden, a couple of days later, we all got permission to go home. This time I didn't go back to my father, but straight home to Mother, I was missing her a lot.

Life under Socialism and After

A brigade arrived from Kazakhstan after the war and I made the acquaintance of a young man. Mother advised me to get married, I was getting on for 25, and soon there wouldn't be anyone to choose from. We had nothing at all when we got married in 1946. Initially we lived in barracks, then a family invited us to move in with them. They only had two beds, the mother slept on the kitchen table.

My husband was a mechanic and soon after got invited to another village where we rented a room. We had two more moves from village to village, mainly for extra pay. My husband was a decent worker, but he was always being lured away to other jobs by the promise of better pay and lodgings. We had two sons, one born in 1947, the other in 1950; we didn't have a nursery in those days so I had to stay at home to look after them. My sons grew up and went their separate ways; one went to college and became an excavation engineer. He was the elder. And the younger also went to college, he became a production engineer. In the last few years I've been living in Ikovka, not far from Kurgan. My husband's dead and I'm alone. All my sisters got a good education; two of them worked as accountants up to retirement, and Lena rose to head a factory department. We all live in different places, but try to meet up at least once a year, as best we can.

I have a small allotment where I grow a few bits and pieces. We used to plough it up, but now we just dig over the soil. I do it all myself these days; but my health's not getting any better. I'll probably do no sowing next year. Even the little bit I did last year is getting too much for me. I don't see well any more; my sight and hearing are going.

It's a hard time for us elderly folk these days, very tough. For instance, when we used to live and work under socialism, things were pretty clear; we seemed to know where we were going. I just don't understand it now. Prices are ridiculous; I just can't live on my pension. I was better off working, life was a darn sight better than now. You don't mind hundreds, but when everything's counted in thousands and thousands you just don't know where you are, you shut your eyes tight.

We used to have state fruit and vegetable stores. You'd go and buy your potatoes there. Now we've got these joint stock companies, or whatever they're called, they've taken over our old shops. They're either empty or you can't afford to buy anything. I don't know whether things will work out or it'll all fall apart. They've stuff for sale, all right, but at what prices, what terrible prices! Do you know what they do? They wait till lots of people gather round, then they put their prices up. There should be a law against it. There's no law and order, just lawlessness. Who gains from it, eh? This isn't market economy, it's sheer swindling.

It was better in the old days. Prices were stable then; they might even knock a bit off, now they keep adding it on. Farming's going downhill, people are slaughtering the cows so you can't get any milk. While a new generation of cattle grows up we'll die from lack of milk. Same with meat. If you slaughter the cattle there'll be nothing to eat, and you just try to produce a new herd quickly. If things continue like this, we'll never get ourselves out of the hole we've dug for ourselves. There's no productivity. Everywhere they're cutting down on the work force, ceasing production.

I was in town recently, visiting my son. He and I went round all the shops trying to get a pair or shoes; I couldn't get either summer or winter footwear. All we could find were Chinese wares, just toy boats which we can hardly go walking in.

The farmers aren't feeding the country. Of course, they work hard, but they can't do much on their own; some are even packing it in altogether. They just don't have the means, no equipment; even if there was machinery, they couldn't afford to buy it. If farmers are going to survive, they'll have to band together, as in the collective farms. They just won't survive on their own. And another thing: the state has stopped caring about its people.

I just don't know how we're going to live.

OKSANA'S STORY

MY GRANDMOTHER told me that my great-grandfather, Alexander Volkov, was born on 13 March 1881 in the village of Sychevo. Besides him, the family had two sons and four daughters. The parents were fairly well-off peasant farmers with a large farm. My great-grandfather could not read or write, since the village had no school; all his life he lived in Sychevo and never even visited the town. He had no profession as such, yet he was a jack of all trades: he would do jobs for the whole village, making wooden forks, rakes and axe handles. He was therefore well known and liked in the village.

He took a wife in 1900, marrying Avdotia Sidorovna. As my grandmother would say, her mother came from a good background, a reasonably wealthy family. Her dowry included cows, sheep and clothing. Her clothes were very grand: sheepskin coat, warm jacket, fur-trimmed overcoat. Great-grandfather brought his young wife into the family house where they stayed together for quite some time, at least until they had three children of their own; then they separated. The father allotted them a separate farmstead. It was there that they managed a sizeable farm: two or three cows, three horses, a pair of oxen, pigs and sheep, and chickens; they farmed about ten hectares.

There were six children in all, but two girls—Yelizaveta and Alexandra—died in infancy, since there was no one to look after them in those days—just one field nurse for the whole region. So they ended up with two sons, the elder Ivan, the younger, Alexander, and two daughters, Maria and Anastasia. Anastasia is my grandmother.

When Ivan had two children of his own, Great-grandfather allotted them land, or partitioned them off, as Grandmother used to say. Their father brought Ivan a fine five-walled house, gave him a horse, cow, sheep and poultry, saying he would have to farm for himself. In 1926, the younger son, Alexander, got married—he was born in 1906. He too got divided off and that is how they lived, Grandmother and her sister, they were still quite young then. Collectivization started in '29.

Grandmother must have been about fifteen. But her memory of those times is still fresh; that's because they were such hard times, full of changes, the entire family got shaken up. That's why it sticks in her memory. She even cries a lot when she talks about it. In '29 when collectivization began, my great-grand-father, Alexander Zakharovich, did not want to join the collective farm and quit his own farm; it was a decent-sized farm, after all, bringing in a decent living. He was always convinced that whoever works well should live well. He used to say you'd get no benefit from lumping good farmers and loafers together.

They told him that if he didn't join the kolkhoz, he would have to meet the grain procurement plan. The first time they set the grain delivery target he met it; then he got a new target, much tougher, yet he still managed to meet it. But when he got the third target, he had nothing left to give. So he was dekulak-ized as an enemy of the people, yet not exiled; they took into account that he had never kept farm labourers—that is, he had run the farm all by himself.

He had 'golden hands', as we say, he was well known and liked in the village: that's why he got off lightly. But they came and confiscated everything, all except the house itself; my grandmother was then 15. At the same time, they dekulakized his younger son, Alexander, Grandmother's brother. He also had a thriving farm; he had settled in well. The farm was sold off for the grain procurement debts, and there was no one to help him, neither his father nor anyone else; so Alexander's family was exiled to Perm Region. Where to exactly Grand-mother doesn't recall.

Grandmother says they knew nothing of his fate for a long time; his father and mother were terribly upset since they had no news whatsoever. They later discovered that he had died there; they heard that from his wife when she came back. She said he had died of starvation, and maybe from constant worry about his family, especially their only son, little Konstantin, who also died in Perm Region. Anyway, as things worked out, Alexander's wife returned to Sychevo only in 1963, and Grand-mother says it had so shattered her life she never married again after that, she never had any more children, and she only returned to Sychevo when she was fairly elderly.

The elder son, Ivan, joined the kolkhoz, unlike Alexander and his father, and he became a brigade leader; but Grand-mother tells me that the father and son, Alexander Zakharovich and Alexander Alexandrovich, were stubborn and pig-headed characters, while Ivan, so she says, had a head on his shoulders, he was a wily old bird. He realized, even foresaw, how things were turning out; that's why he joined up after his father and Alexander were dekulakized. Work was indescribably tough and he frequently had to sleep in the open air. Grandmother says he had to guard grain at the threshing floor right in the open, come rain, snow, frost, whatever. Evidently that's how Ivan caught a chill. They did suggest he go for an operation, but he would have had to give up his calf for that. But since he had no farm of his own and could hardly look after his family—and they had five children by then—he had to forgo the operation. You didn't get sick notes in those days, and he had to go to work utterly worn out and sick. There was no alternative since they were likely to brand you a backslider. They could even have you done for being an enemy of the people.

He literally worked till he dropped, and when they carried him home he died within three days. Grandmother remembers it well. After being dekulakized, my great-grandfather also joined the kolkhoz since he now had no choice; he had to live somehow. My great-grandmother also had to do her bit; up till then she had never worked in the fields, having so much to do at home. Initially, Great-grandfather had a job in the stables, and then got made a 'high grade worker'—what they now call an agronomist, someone responsible for the sowing.

His wife suffered a good deal over her sons: Ivan had died, leaving five little children; and when she had no word from Alexander it all piled up on her, she went through hell, her life was turned upside down. There was nothing to eat; kolkhoz workers received 200 grams each of ersatz food per labour day —ersatz was rather like mixed animal fodder, from which they would bake rolls. Great-grandmother suffered terribly, moaning and groaning constantly, and in 1938 she became paralysed. It seems that she recovered somewhat, got up from her sick bed, began to walk about and appeared to be as right as rain; but then something went wrong with her head, she went off her rocker, some say, or she didn't quite... I don't know how to say it. Upstairs things weren't quite right. She was always saying she had stayed long enough, now had to go home, her old man would be angry with her, the farm had been left unattended. Then she would get up, gather her belongings together into a bundle and wander about the countryside. She could spend all day wandering about before someone would lead her home, insisting that this was her home.

She died in 1958 and even my mother recalls taking her out for walks in the village and having to listen to her complaints that there were no real farmers on the land, the land had no master.

My great-grandfather's eldest daughter, Anastasia, my grandmother, was born in 1913. She was the fifth child in the family and she managed to complete one class of the four-year school; then her father took her away from school since she had to do some spinning, so he said, and bring something into the house. Inasmuch as every member of the family had some job or other, Grandmother had no choice in the matter; that was her duty.

My grandmother married in 1932. She ran away to marry, as she puts it. My mother tells me that our grandmother was very headstrong, wilful, evidently taking after Grandfather. Well, she ran away and got married to Ivan Gusev who was a cobbler. He was a good worker, but a bit of a rowdy; that's why he ended up as a mere cobbler. Grandmother, though, had always had a roof over her head and lived comfortably enough; but now she had hooked up with someone below her. Once she was married she left home, but was soon back with her husband, throwing themselves on the mercy of her father. They begged his forgiveness, and he pardoned them; he was fond of and sorry for his daughter. In the end he gave his daughter two sheep as a dowry. For the time that was regarded as a fair gift; he had no farm and nothing to his name by then. These were the collectivization years.

Grandmother went to live with her husband and, in 1937, they had a son, Dmitri, who died of scarlet fever when he was a year and one month old. As Grandmother says, he died for want of a doctor or anyone to cure him. A second son, also Dmitri, was born in 1941 and when he was only one month ten days old, his father had to go to the front. A year later they received notification that he was missing, presumed killed, so throughout the war Grandmother toiled on the railways, leaving the child with his grandfather on the father's side. For her work she would get 600 grams of bread for herself and 300 grams for a dependent. All through the war she also kept a cow and a vegetable garden, so managed to stave off the worst of the war years; it was easier in the countryside than in town. She even helped out her next-door neighbour who had been left with three children, and who had only a tiny garden. All the same, they were dreadful times.

Grandmother married again in 1946. My mother says she really was a courageous woman, since she took her second husband into her first husband's father's house. The mother-in-law was initially against it, but then she grew to treat the second husband like her own son. There was a daughter from this marriage, Galina. That is my mother. All her life Grandmother was grateful to the father of her first husband, a very good man; he it was who helped her keep body and soul together, took in her second husband, and was generally a genuinely nice man.

My grandmother is religious. She always says that people should have something sacred, something to believe in. I'm used to seeing her sitting down at table, saying grace, praying when she goes to bed, all the time. She travels to church at Smolino. Not as often as she would like, perhaps, but she does go.

Grandmother's younger sister, Maria, was born in 1916 and had four years of schooling, in the same village. At that time education was extremely good and she went on to a job as secretary in the village council; from there she became an accountant and a cafe manageress; my grandmother regards her as a very educated woman. She married in 1939 and went off to live in the neighbouring village of Vvedenskoe. There she worked at the military headquarters. All her life she kept a farm, and still does. True, it's not very grand these days since she hasn't the strength any more, but she keeps cows and chickens. Her husband came through the war; they've three children: Vera, Nina and Galina. Two of them went to university. Galina is a gynaecologist in Moscow. Vera is a research fellow in maths and physics, works and lives in Saratov. And the youngest daughter, Nina, has been disabled since birth.

My grandmother lost her second husband in 1950; he died of his war wounds, leaving her with the two children: her elder son Dima and my mother, Galya. She switched jobs and went to work in the disabled institution in the village of Logovushka, about six kilometres from Sychevo. Things got worse for her, she recalls, in the 1950s when she was barred from keeping the cow and had her vegetable garden taken away; they began to plough up her garden and force them all into kolkhoz. Those who were not members of the kolkhoz, yet were living in the village, had their gardens confiscated since they no longer had rights to such gardens. So there was Grandmother working at the disabled institution and earning no more than 350 roubles a month in old money—that's only 35 roubles in new money—and getting a pension of 400 roubles for the kids.

She was a nurse by this time. All the same she lived much better on this paltry sum than the kolkhozniks, who received next to nothing on the farm for their labour days. That's why she wasn't at all keen on joining the kolkhoz: she knew full well that nothing good would come out of it. And she never changed her view. She stubbornly refused to change her job, remaining at the institution. She says she doesn't know what would have happened to me and the children whose fathers had died in the war if it had not been for our great-grandfather on her first husband's side. I've already mentioned him before. Anyway, Grandmother kept out of the kolkhoz.

My Parents

My mother is Galina, she was born in 1947 in the same village where Grandmother had been born. She went to the eight-year school in Sychevo, and then went on to complete her schooling at Vvedenskoe. Mother tells me that she had country ways instilled in her as a young girl: she could milk a cow, clean out the cow-sheds, feed the pigs, mow hay, prepare logs for winter and do all the heavy chores; in any case Mother had no one to help out. On completing eight years of schooling, she carried on her education with Grandmother's assistance. If it had not been for her, further schooling would have been out of the question.

Mother recalls that things got really difficult with bread in about 1960. At that time Mother was going to school at Vvedenskoe where ration cards were given out; but she didn't get any since she came from Sychevo; and she didn't get any at Sychevo since she was studying in Vvedenskoe! She was staying in a hostel then and remained without any bread. Times were very tough. In those times a residence permit meant everything.

Mother well remembers Andrei Kuntsev who was the class tutor. It was through his good offices that the matter was brought before the education council which authorized her to receive a bread roll from the school canteen each day. She owes a lot to that man in becoming a school teacher. He it was who had a considerable influence on her. After secondary school she went to college to study history and languages and, in 1965, graduated, then got married. Since her husband, my father, still had two years of his course to go, she came back to the village to live with Grandmother. My father then gained an engineering degree, while she was teaching at school. She taught literature, drawing and physical education. In 1970, her eldest daughter, Oksana, was born—that's me. Realizing that it would be very hard for daughter and husband to get by, Grandmother again went to work in the disabled institution, even though she was an old-age pensioner by then.

My father, Vladimir Nikrylov, was born on 29 February 1944. He was from the Voronezh Region. His parents had worked in industry and, as he was always telling us, he was the son of a communist who had joined the Party in 1924. In other words, his father joined the Party at the appeal on Lenin's death in 1924.

His family had six children. The eldest daughter was about fifteen years older than my father. She had come from Kurgan and got married; Grandfather had sent my father to his elder sister for her to keep an eye on him. So Dad arrived from Kurgan, found a job and then gained admission to the Kurgan Engineering College which he graduated from in 1971. The next year he started work at a chemical engineering plant making goods for the armed forces; at the same time he joined the Party; as he would say, he joined up out of his convictions, as the son of a communist, as a second generation Party man. He still regards himself a communist. Even when the new authorities banned the Party, he still kept his Party card at home, along with the rest of his documents.

Our family left for Kurgan in 1971 because Dad had graduated and started work there. At the present time my father is chief designer at the Armature Works, while Mother is teaching Russian and literature at a city school.

I regard Kurgan as my home town, though I don't think I'd like to spend all my life here; I might well leave for another city. I enjoy travel.

I don't want to leave Russia. I might accept going to work abroad for a time, but not forever. I couldn't accept that, if only because I treasure the feeling of patriotism developed in us. I just could not imagine living anywhere else.

I think that somehow Russia has to find its own way, since no other country in the world has had such a history; nothing's going to come of simply copying the economic system of capitalist countries. They have different conditions, different reasons, different developments. You can't get away from considering all the natural laws of development, and going your own way. Mind you, there is no going back to the past, of course. It's not worth it.

The papers are today full of rehabilitation of the kulaks and returning them their land. Mother always says that the land ought to be worked by those who love it. And love for the land does not come easy; it has to be cultivated in people who work the land. She says that since we haven't lived in the countryside for some time, we no longer have our roots there. Even if they gave her land she would not be able to work it. She doesn't have the strength, nor the conditions and so on. She has no intention of claiming Grandfather's land, or that of Great-grand-father or anyone else. Land ought to go to those who are working on it, who live on it, who love it, simply because each person should have his own niche in life.

I agree with her because I was born in the town and regard myself as a town dweller. I am not accustomed to country life and could never work on the land. My destiny is quite different.

IRINA CH.

IRINA was born in 1968, a time now labelled the era of stagnation. Yet it was a time of stability as well. There may not have been much food in the shops, but everyone had ration coupons which ensure them monthly provisions—200 grams of butter, one kilogram of salami and of flour, etc.

Irina's forbears on her father's and mother's side had been 'dekulakized' because her family had never supported the communist régime. Although they had never talked openly of their opposition, Irina had understood from relatives that they did not believe in the communist ideology taught them in school. As a child, Irina naturally went to nursery and school, yet she had always sensed a skeleton in the family closet. Finally, she summoned up the courage to ask her grandmother to tell her about the past; it was then that she discovered the awful truth about collectivization.

That happened some time before perestroika, so accounts by historians that appeared in the early 1990s came as no surprise. She was eager to give an interview and responded to all questions openly and honestly. She has no fear of the KGB, unlike her parents; nor does she fear exile, unlike her grandmother.

It is her fervent hope that by uncovering the past she will help people to avoid mistakes in the future. She loves Russia and would like to find happiness in her own country.

Irina's story

My Forbears

My ancestors on both my mother's and father's side were wealthy peasants. The head of my mother's family, Grigory, was born in the Polovinki Region in 1880. When he was a young man he worked as steward in a merchant's house. His employer had confidence in him thanks to his diligence and quick wits, and in time Grigory married the merchant's daughter and inherited the business—a factory, several houses and cattle. Family members recall that he was religious and went to a church school; he died at the early age of 40—so at least was spared eviction.

Grigory's wife Praskovya, however, suffered all the hardship that eviction brought. She was the same age as her husband, so was 50 at the time of 'dekulakization'. She had no education to speak of, was religious and gave birth to five children—three boys and two girls. For twelve years she had brought up the children by herself, while coping with the business.

When collectivization began in 1930, all her property was confiscated, including even her linen. She and her two youngest children were sent into exile in the Perm Region for three years, which she described as resembling hell. It is hard to say what helped this woman to survive, whether her belief in God or her motherly devotion to her children. She was allowed to return to Kurgan in 1933, but her health was ruined and she died within a year.

Her daughters Zoya and Praskovya had not been evicted because they had married poor peasants. During the collectivization years, such marriages were very common and helped some members of wealthy families to escape death and repression. Zoya and Praskovya, however, could not live and work on a collective farm, so they moved to the town where the elder sister did odd jobs, while the younger worked as a shop assistant. Both had had a primary education, believed in God and, during the war years (1941-45), they did war work; all their lives they hoped for better and happier times, but did not live to see them.

90

The eldest son, Ivan, was born in 1909. At the time of eviction he was married and had his own household; he and his family were despatched to the Sverdlovsk Region in 1930. Two years later he was back in Kurgan and, like his mother, tried to adapt himself to the Soviet régime. His period of exile had killed in him any desire to resist or put up a struggle. He felt that only lies and cunning would enable him to survive. Thanks to such qualities he managed to gain an administrative post and changed jobs several times, always retaining a supervisory position.

Alexander and Vasily, the two other brothers, endured the hardship of exile together with their mother. After her death, they lived at their sister's house before Alexander joined the army as a driver; in 1941, with the outbreak of war, he transported shells at the front; despite many close shaves, he survived the war and upon demobilization travelled to an army friend in Kazakhstan where he worked as a driver until retirement.

Vasily, my grandfather, was born in 1917. He was the youngest son in the family. On qualifying as a high-grade carpenter he found work in that trade precarious and frequently changed jobs in order to earn a living. He worked at a meat plant and in a vegetable storage depot, and did a number of odd jobs. Since his health had been impaired while in exile, he was not called up when war came, but operated behind the line. In 1944, he married Yekaterina (born 1915) who had been born in a Cossack village in Kazakhstan. As her family had not been wealthy, she did not suffer repression and was active in politics—in campaigns against religion, illiteracy, and so on. After finishing secondary school, she had worked as a bookkeeper and a clerk. Unlike her husband, she had joined the Party, but lost her membership for refusing to take part in harvesting. Fortunately for her, she suffered no further punishment. All the same, the family decided to move and left Kazakhstan for Kurgan where Vasily built them a house. Following the war, they had three children.

The youngest son, Victor (born 1952) went into engineering, graduating from an engineering institute and starting work at a military plant evacuated to Kurgan during wartime. He worked his way up to become departmental chief. He also joined the Party. His wife, who completed higher education, bore him two children. Their daughter Lyubov did a correspondence course in engineering; on graduation she was sent to Vladivostok where she worked and improved her qualifications. She is currently employed as a civil engineer in the port of Vladivostok. She is unmarried and has never joined the Party.

My mother, the eldest daughter Vera, was born in 1947. After completing secondary school she went to work at the local factory. Then her love of reading encouraged her to take a librarianship course and become a librarian. She grew up in the house built by her father and, in 1969, brought her husband, Alexander, to live in the house. They had been neighbours before the wedding and grown up together in the same neighbourhood. Alexander's grandfather Anfim (born in 1890) also suffered eviction. He had owned his own house in the village of Kolesnikovo; he also possessed an oil mill and a small business. Insofar as he was not very wealthy he could not afford to hire any farmhands; one might best describe him as a medium peasant. That did not stop him from suffering repression: his house and property were confiscated and he was exiled to the northern Urals. In 1935 he returned from exile, but went to live in the town rather than in his old village. Anfim had three children from his first marriage and two from his second.

So the village had lost seven workers.

Anfim built himself a house in the town where he and his wife brought up their children. He maintained that he always wanted to bring up his children to love the countryside and produce good harvests; but the régime needed hired workers rather than peasant proprietors. Although the family had not suffered repression, like other evicted families, distress and anguish turned the men to drink. Both Anfim and his wife were religious, but they had to suffer much pressure from the régime to change their belief to communism and Stalin. Anfim died just after the war from alcoholism. His wife Agapeya lived until 1974. As her relatives recollect, her husband had always despised all communists and never regarded their government as legitimate.

Their elder daughter Anna was born in 1924. Throughout her life she lived in Kurgan and worked as a bookkeeper. Both she and her husband were non-believers, yet Anna inherited her mother's strict moral views. Anna adopted a young boy and brought him up as well as any real mother. Anfim's and Agapeya's son, Ivan, my grandfather (my father's father) was born in 1926 and spent the early years of his life in exile. He doesn't remember the family house and did not work and live, as his father had, in the countryside; he took employment as a foundry worker at a farm machine plant, toiling twelve to fourteen hours a day. He had only completed seven years of schooling. He served in the army in the war and, following it, he got married. His wife, Natalya, was employed at the same farm machine plant, first as a manual worker, then as accountant. They had two children—Alexander and Anatoly.

Eventually, after many years of exhausting labour, Ivan and Natalya had saved up enough to buy a two-room cooperative apartment. Unfortunately, like his father, Ivan took to drink and died at the age of 56 of an industrial disease. Neither Ivan, nor Natalya ever joined the Party; nor did they believe in God. They might be described as the sort of people on whose behalf the communists had proclaimed their slogans and their raison d'être, without producing anything more than resolutions and proclamations.

Ivan's and Natalya's eldest son, Anatoly (born 1950), gained a full secondary education and became a foundry worker like his father. In his spare time he does a good deal of hunting and fishing which enables him to supply the family with fresh fish and meat. Anatoly's first marriage ended in divorce; his son, Yevgeny, grew up fatherless, entered the Suvorov Military School and went on to a military academy. In other words, the state brought him up and supplied him with all his needs instead of his father. In return, however, it demanded complete obedience and readiness to make sacrifices.

Anatoly's second marriage resulted in two children who are both currently at school.

Ivan's and Natalya's younger son, Alexander, is my father. He completed a secondary education, obtained a driving licence and subsequently worked as a driver. After marrying his sweetheart Vera, the two moved into the house of Vera's father; it was only in 1980 that they had enough money to put down their first payment for a cooperative apartment. My parents have never been Party members, nor believed in communism or communist slogans. At first they welcomed perestroika, but soon became disillusioned because of the lack of any real change in their lives.

In the early years of their marriage, they had frequent disputes and debates, but later apathy set in. They bickered over the family finances: for ten years they made regular payments for their apartment, which drained their resources and prevented them from realizing their dream of becoming reasonably well-off. However, as prices increased, their living standard declined; all the same, they still hope for a change for the better, for economic reform and genuine improvements from the present government. The factory where my father works is to distribute shares to its workers which he hopes will bring some tangible results.

When asked 'How would you have lived if there had been no revolution in Russia?', my mother replied that they would have been farmers in their old village. Even today they would be keen to live and work in the country, although they appreciate that they have lost all farming skills. In any case, they have read and heard about all the obstacles in the way of modern farmers—lack of technology and equipment, no credit facilities, the hostility of many collective farmers to private land ownership, etc. That is why it is highly unlikely that their dreams will ever be realized.

During the collectivization years, the communist régime eliminated the entire class of proprietors and severed all generational ties. It broke all labour and cultural traditions in terms of father to son, mother to daughter succession.

If the children of evicted farmers had returned to their parents' farms and had developed the necessary farming skills, their grandchildren and great-grandchildren might have become farmers; as it is, the children did not return, and the children's children are now unlikely ever to become farmers.

My parents have two children. I was born in 1970, my brother Maxim in 1981, already in the new apartment. I still remember the house which my grandfather built. Three generations lived there and, on occasion, as many as twenty people would gather round the dinner table. The family had been very happy, with all duties divided into men's and women's responsibilities. That is why there were never any conflicts. The women cooked, washed, did the housework; the men fetched water from the well, chopped firewood and tilled the land.

They had been on the best of terms with their neighbours, married in the locality, as Irina's mother had done, and often helped each other out. In other words, they lived a typical village life while residing in the town.

Irina Ch.

On the outskirts of town, people's lives differed little from those in the countryside. The only difference was that they tended to work in heavy industry, not on a collective farm. I did not know what starvation was, since food was reasonably plentiful during the Brezhnev years. Although there were few luxuries available, milk and meat products and bread and cakes were in good supply for all families. The children's needs were relatively modest since they had never known a life of luxury.

When I was six months old my parents took me to a day nursery and then, later, to the kindergarten where I was taught to think and behave more as a member of a collective than as an individual. My mother had taught me to read early, but I do not recall my first book. Although there were few books in my parent's house, my mother was a keen reader out of both personal and professional interests. I learned about her evicted relatives in early childhood, which is why the later exposure of the Communist Party following the perestroika period did not come as a surprise. At school and college I had been a member of the Young Communist League (Komsomol), although I disliked Komsomol-organized social work and did what I could to avoid it. I did not enjoy my time at school, my relations with the teachers were not particularly friendly.

My teachers taught in a very formal fashion. I had neither a favourite subject, nor a favourite teacher. Being a fairly quiet, unflappable girl, I had no disciplinary problems. I am evidently fairly phlegmatic and not a good mixer, inheriting these characteristics from my reticent father. My mother is the driving force of the family, brimming with ideas and the power behind her husband.

The role distribution is typical of many Russian families where the man is unable to keep the family on his income, which is why the wife is frequently the head of the family.

I made my own choice of higher education, though influenced by my mother. After secondary school I did foreign languages at a teacher-training institute. Since the entry examination was fairly easy, I had no difficulty finding a place. My student years coincided with the perestroika years. Even so, little altered at the institute. The only exceptions were that the Komsomol ceased to hold meetings and the lecturers tended to mellow somewhat. I have never taken an interest in politics. My favourite tutors were those who had been at the Institute for twenty years or more; they were the ones who gave the most interesting lectures and were more qualified and cultured in all aspects of life.

On the whole, I am dissatisfied with my level of knowledge, though I blame nobody but myself. Until recently the institute had ensured employment for its graduates by directing them to various schools. I therefore thought I would have no trouble finding a teaching position. However, from 1992 graduates have had to seek vacant posts themselves, which is easier for the better students than for those with lower grades. My problem is that my reticence let me down during my first school practice period; I had been unable to establish close contact with my pupils and had decided that I would never make a good teacher. It is virtually impossible to find an interpreting job in a small town, and I confess that I have no gift for business or commerce. In fact, I would like to take after my great-grand-father—a thoroughly uncommon aspiration for a young woman of today, especially as the authorities do not pay compensation to repressed families. I think the future is so uncertain.

TATIANA P.

TATIANA'S relatives on her father's and mother's side had been well-to-do peasants. They had not suffered severe repression, like many of their countrymen, since they had managed to move house in time. That is probably why their four relatively happy families live on in the countryside, building their homes, working the land and never imagining life away from mother nature.

Tatiana is a second-generation townsperson. Her mother was born in the countryside and moved to town when she married. Tatiana's childhood was mainly in the 1970s, so her adolescence coincided with perestroika. In talking of the changes associated with perestroika, she mentioned one factor above all others: freedom to seek work of her choice.

She gives the impression of a person who has already found her way in life and has great faith in the future. I interviewed her in the town apartment which she shares with her parents and brother. The apartment is fairly standard, yet the woman's touch had clearly given it a cosy and individual atmosphere.

Tatiana's parents still dream of their plot of land, yet seem fairly happy with their small dacha allotment. As for Tatiana herself, she has no desire to live in the countryside; she is not used to farming and has thoughts only of becoming an interpreter in the city. All the same, she seems to have inherited from her family the qualities of diligence, integrity and an independent spirit. It is my hope that these traits will help her achieve her goal in these troubled times.

Tatiana's story

Mother's Family

I heard of my mother's family from Grandfather Kornei.

My great-grandfather was born in 1870 in the village of Yelovatka, Saratov Province. They had a fairly substantial farmstead, up to fifty desyatins,[1] a dozen or so horses and cattle, and a number of hired labourers. Anyway, they worked the land and had livestock. My great-grandfather then married my great-grandmother and they began to run the farm as a family concern.

Life went on in the village without much change until round about 1931 when collectivization started; they received a visit from some Komsomol enthusiasts who worked on the kolkhoz. In short, the requisitioners took all they had: chickens, ducks, cows, the lot. There was even some government resolution forcing them to pay extortionate taxes, even though they had nothing but the shirts on their backs. They got by somehow, Goodness knows how. They did not suffer exile, but life was pretty tough since the entire farmstead had been completely pillaged.

All the same, they refused to join the kolkhoz!

They had no real idea what was happening. Everything worthwhile had been confiscated—there were no exceptions—so they could hardly claim victimization by the authorities; somehow they got on with their lives on their own. Their intention was to start all over again, but that turned out to be too difficult; so they decided to pack up and leave. They moved somewhere in Perm Province and set up house there. That was in 1933.

Granddad Kornei was an only son, which was quite untypical of the time. He went to school in Perm Province, but when the time came for him to join the Komsomol, when he was 14, he was turned down as a kulak's son. Evidently, a

---

[1]A *desyatin* (Russian: *desyatina*) is an old Russian land measure equivalent to 2.7 acres.

fellow revealed that he had recognized him as the son of a farmer who had hired the man as a farmhand.

My great-grandmother was illiterate, but she was keen for her son to get on in life. She gave him all her spare time and a great deal of affection. Even before 1917 my great-grandfather had sold his house and put some five thousand roubles by for a rainy day; yet the new authorities confiscated the lot. Goodness knows where the savings went!

When Great-granddad was in Perm Province, he was eager to get started all over again. But taxation wore the family down: since Great-granddad had nothing, he could pay nothing and he ended up, along with all the men, in prison—four months in gaol for non-payment of taxes. After that, they moved house again to distance themselves as far as possible from persecution. That is how they ended up here in Petukhovo, Kurgan Region.

They managed to build a new house and got by reasonably well; it was not long before they started up a small farm and a market garden. They now stayed put, living here until Great-granddad died in 1946, and Great-grandma in 1955. My granddad finished the Petukhov school and, when war broke out in 1941, he was 24.

While he was still in Petukhovo, he learned to be a driver, so that during the war he transported the wounded. I don't remember exactly where it was, but a village suffered pretty heavy bombing and he got his first wound. A shell splinter caught him in the eye and he had to spend time in hospital before being sent back to the front. Round about 1943 he got another wound, this time in the leg and had to be invalided out of the army. He spent ages in hospital, in some place by the name of Kozelsk, though I don't know what region; then he came home. Soon after he was assigned duties in the rear.

When he came home to his parents, he did bits and pieces as soon as he was reasonably fit. All his life he had worked with cars, so the trade always came in handy. He got married in Petukhovo to my grandma: her name was Anna, and she's still alive.

Grandma was born in 1924, in north Kazakhstan, not that far from Petukhovo. When war broke out, her family decided to move away; it was quite a sizeable family and, while Great-granddad was away in the war, they all came to Petukhovo where they had some distant relative. They felt it would be easier to live somewhere all together; so the whole lot moved here.

My grandma went to school till she was fifteen, and a good pupil she was too. She still helps the kids with their reading and arithmetic, constantly setting them homework.

While she was bringing up her children she never had a job outside the house, at least not until they could walk and look after themselves. It was sometime after the war, I can't recall when exactly, in 1950 or maybe 1955, that she took a job as accountant in Petukhovo after taking her accountancy exams. One reason was that Granddad was unable to work for long; he retired early on a disability pension. So someone had to keep the family.

Both of them now live in Petukhovo and keep a small homestead: a cow, chickens, ducks and an orchard. I do what I can to visit them a couple of times a year. They are both keenly interested in politics. Grandma seems to weigh it all up calmly, she understands what's going on: you can't turn the clock back, can't change the way things are. As for Granddad, he's an incurable optimist, full of enthusiasm for perestroika, heart and soul.

What I mean is that he was glad it all happened, though he still has a bone to pick with the communists for what they did to his parents. That's why he is a Yeltsin man.

Uncle Victor is my Granddad's and Grandma's eldest son. He was born in Petukhovo in 1945 and completed his schooling there. He has never moved, not even given it a thought. After school, he did an apprenticeship at a meat processing plant where he still works.

He has a fairly large family—three children. He had a big house built recently and does a bit of farming on the side. You could say that his family is repeating the lives of their parents. His wife has no job at the moment partly because she has few qualifications. She used to work as a technical assistant, but when the plant was modernized or, rather, slimmed down, she was 'slimmed down' as well and became redundant, though she gets some welfare assistance.

Granddad and Grandma had four children all told. Next in line is Auntie Lyuda who was also born in the village, left school at 17, went to college and became an electrical engineer. Her first job was as an electrician in Petukhovo, but then she changed jobs to become a laboratory assistant since she couldn't get a job as an electrician; now she is employed as a senior laboratory technician at the Petukhovo State Inspection Service. She is married with two children.

My Uncle Valera was born in 1961. He did eight classes at school and went on to college to become a fitter. All in Petukhovo. When he received his fitter's diploma he went straight into the army; he served his time and came home, taking a driving job. He is still working as a driver, now doing long-distance runs all over the place. He and his wife and two children are still living with Granddad and Grandma.

His wife graduated from Omsk Technical College and is now involved in garment making for a cooperative that she and her husband have started up. She even does a lot of her work at home. At the same time, she and Uncle Valera keep a few animals and are working with their parents to build a house for themselves: the roof and walls are all up, though they still have the inside to finish off. Still, it shouldn't be long before they move in.

My mother was born in 1946; she went to school in Petukhovo, completing ten grades. After that she fancied going to agricultural college, I've no idea why, I suppose she had some interest in farming. Then she came to Kurgan. She had a good friend here, which is probably why she came. One thing's for sure: she hankered after life in the town: 'It's no life for a girl in the village,' she'd say. So she came, went to college and graduated as a zoologist (I think). And then she went back to Petukhovo. It so happened that my dad went there looking for her, I'm not sure how it all turned out, but he came and took her back to Kurgan.

Once in Kurgan, she got a job in a bakery doing menial jobs, but you can imagine the pay was pretty poor, not enough to keep us. So she upped and went to a poultry plant and works there as a zoologist even now.

My Father's Family

My great-grandmother was born in 1875. Her name was Anastasia. She was pretty poor and totally illiterate. My great-grandfather, Semyon, was born in 1869; he was reasonably secure, working as a lumberjack. He had his own fairly substantial house in the Kirov Region. And that's where they lived fairly comfortably. It was a two-storied building. I well recall Grandmother telling me about it: the house was in a forest, in a beautiful part of the country. They ran a small farmstead, even had servants and lots and lots of children.

There are probably about six still living; another four died. So they must have had about ten children. Those that died did so very young.

Great-grandfather lived in the same house all his life, till 1935; the communists did not touch him for the simple reason that his house was deep in the forest. My great-grandmother had died before the Revolution, so Great-grandfather had to look after all the children himself and run the homestead. He never married again. As the children grew up, one by one they left the village. Tamara got married there, but since her husband was from Vyatka, she went off with him eventually. I don't think she ever worked—her husband kept her.

Zoya married a solicitor and went off to Cheboksary; she too stayed at home, bringing up her children. Granddad Ivan graduated from a Moscow medical institute and now lives there with his family.

My grandmother was born in 1916. She doesn't remember her mother; starvation was pretty common and terrible just before the Revolution, but she survived it, had her children, and then died. But Grandma remembers her father very well and is always telling me about him and how much he did for his family.

He was hard-working, kind and generous with the children, all the time helping them, teaching them about life and work, so that when they left home they could stand on their own two feet.

I don't know why, but Grandma left her village, I think to go to school, and she lived for a while in Kirov, then somewhere else. At first she went to Yelutorovsk to study and entered medical college, to become a midwife. Then she moved to us in Kurgan Region, since her sister Zoya had made her way here.

Our grandmother is the youngest of her family, they are all dead and she's the only one left. It was quite a bit later, just before the war, that she ran into my grandfather, Nikolai, born in 1915, and they got married. After the marriage they initially lived in Kurgan; then, when my father was born in 1939, they felt that war was in the offing and Granddad took Grandma off to his mother's grandfather. That's how they ended up in the Ukraine.

When they left they took all their possessions with them, things like furniture, anything worth taking, so that they could start a new life in their new home. But war broke out after they had been there for only two years. Granddad had to go to the front, the Nazis were advancing on their town, so they had to be evacuated quickly. They had a pretty torrid time of it, especially when the bombing raids began. Grandma told me how she had to rush with my dad—he was only two at the time—into some shop and she only just made it in time as the bombs came down. A bomb landed right on the shop where all the people were sheltering; you can imagine the dreadful carnage when it went off. But Grandma and Dad emerged unscathed. However, Grandma soon decided to get back to Kurgan with her son. It took them ever such a long time; they spent a couple of weeks on freight trains, living in cattle wagons; they were crammed full of refugees; and all the time planes were flying overhead protecting the freight trains. While they were on the road, my dad fell ill, he had pneumonia. I've no idea how he survived: times were tough, it was very cold and everywhere was filthy. But they made it to Kurgan somehow.

They brought with them my granddad's mother-in-law. Grandma got herself a job in Kurgan and left her son to the safe keeping of the mother-in-law. She worked on the railways, helping out with the medical trains, since she had had some medical training.

After the war Granddad returned. I don't know what happened, but they divorced shortly after, and Grandma didn't marry again; she just lived with my father, her son, and Granddad went and married some other woman; he had no more children. So now Granddad and Grandma were living apart. Grandma took a job as midwife after the war, in the railway clinic. She worked there 46 years. Even so, she still doesn't have her own apartment, she lives in one room in a communal flat, sharing a kitchen.

Religion and My Relatives

My mother's grandmother was always very God-fearing, always believed in God and was very religious, going to church regularly, saying grace before each meal, and asking God to forgive all our trespasses. As for my great-grandfather, I cannot say he believed much in religion, nor can I say he was not religious.

My granddad was born in 1917, went to school under the Soviet régime, tried to do what other lads did—and young people at the time were all against God; so that's why he did not believe. Yet nowadays something seems to have happened to him and he says he believes in God, I'm not sure how much. He reckons that God is always thinking of us, God does so much good for us, always helps us when we are in need. From what he says it would seem he has been converted.

As for Grandma, I cannot say her faith is that strong, but she believes in God in her own way. Since her village has no church, she naturally does not go to church. On my father's side, both Great-grandmother and Great-grandfather used to go with their entire family to the local church close to Kirov Province. Their elder children kept up the tradition and now have icons at home, and special little altars in the corner where they cross themselves and say their prayers. Grandmother remains a believer to this day, and still goes to church regularly.

My mother was baptized, although she is not much of a believer these days; my dad is an atheist, he doesn't believe in anything. My own attitude to religion is a bit complex. When I was a Young Pioneer and in the Komsomol I got by all right without religion. And nothing bad happened. Now I read a lot, books and articles, and I am starting to realize that people always used to believe in God, seemed to thrive on it and they were not evil for doing so.

I have been to our local church; I'm glad it has been restored. I first went to church in Kiev when I was at school. Mother and I made a trip to Kiev; what a lovely place it is too. Then we had an excursion a couple of years ago round old Russian towns—Suzdal and Rostov and so on, where there are many churches. That made quite an impression on me; I found it absolutely fascinating. I've come to the conclusion that no one should ban religion since so many people believe in God.

My Parents

Dad wanted to be a doctor after the war. So he went off to a medical college in Kirov since Kurgan had none. He took his entrance examinations, but failed miserably so had to return home and enlist for the armed forces. Luckily for him, he was not conscripted owing to high blood pressure—at the time it was not that hard to get out of military service. When he returned from the medical, he enrolled in the Kurgan Engineering Institute and went on to become a fully-qualified engineer. At the same time, he did some army training in the Military Faculty at the Institute and, when he graduated, he was both an engineer and a lieutenant. He then found employment in Institution 83/1—i.e. a labour colony, where he still works as engineer.

My parents married in 1970, and Dad brought Mother from the countryside to Kurgan. They first lived with my grandmother, in a single room with communal kitchen; but when I was born that made four of us in the tiny room. We spent three years there. It wasn't long, yet I can remember it well: a two-storied block, two entrances, wooden house, probably some forty years old. It was ages before it had central heating put in, not before 1985. We had to fuel the furnaces with wood. Not long ago they had major repairs to the house and linked it up with the municipal water system—but there's still no hot water, and the cold tap lets out just a trickle. Central heating is all there is in the way of 'luxury'. No toilet, no bathroom. And we're talking about 1985!

Our neighbours were a married couple and their two children—with two rooms between them. We all got on reasonably well and helped each other out when necessary. There were never any serious arguments. We stayed on until 1974 and then Dad received a two-roomed flat from his workplace. That's why he had taken a job in the colony, so that he could obtain an apartment.

We moved into the new apartment where my brother was born, in 1974. I was about 12 when Dad got a three-roomed apartment; since then I've had my own room. For the house move we bought a complete set of new furniture, a comfortable settee, washing machine, dresser, new colour television—so our circumstances had changed for the better. That was before perestroika; it would be much harder to do these days.

Grannie was left with all the old furniture: dressing table, an ancient television set, I've no idea what year it was made, battered old sofa, quite cosy, wooden bookshelf and round wooden table. It's all still there. Nothing has changed with her furniture. The old chest of drawers is still there, though painted up a bit. She has no desire to give any of it away, nor does she want to buy anything new—it's all a reminder of the past.

We have lots of books, virtually our own library, with books lining the walls in three rows. I couldn't say how many we've got. But they line the walls in my room as well as in the living room. I'm very fond of history books, and novels as well. I like all the books Mum collects; she doesn't simply collect books, she loves reading them. We have books on history, on the war, history of Russia generally, detective novels.

It's Mother who does most of the housework—cleaning, washing and that sort of thing. I try to give her a hand when I can: she does the washing, I do the cleaning, and she's responsible for the cooking when I'm busy. On the whole, we tend to do things by halves. As for my father, he spends a lot of his time at the dacha.

We've had our dacha for the past eleven years; it isn't far from our flat. When we bought it everything was already there, all the plants and flowers were sown. But all there was on the site was a tiny shed. So when we moved, Dad straightaway built a house, then a bathhouse and a greenhouse. Anyway, he completely fitted it all out. He's good around the house: insulating the windows or the balcony, purely male things. He certainly doesn't do the washing up. I don't think that's altogether fair.

I think men and women should share chores. The woman in the family just doesn't have time to do everything herself; she has to have a rest now and then. It just puts a lot of pressure on her otherwise. In other words, I reckon that the man in the family should give a hand.

When Grandma comes round, she is the one to do the cooking, feeding my parents at lunch and dinner. Mother just cooks breakfast, though she does the cooking on Saturdays and Sundays. As a matter of fact, Dad is quite a good cook. But he only does it when he's in the mood and when there's nothing to eat, when Mother isn't home. Now that I'm grown up I can do the cooking, and I often do. My gran taught me when I was living with her; I spent a lot of time with her when I was little and Mother was out to work. It was Gran who taught me everything.

About Myself

Up to three years old I was at home with Grandma, then I got a place in nursery school. When my brother was born it was hard for Gran to look after the two of us, so I went to nursery and quite enjoyed it.

I learned to read at home and in nursery from the age of three. Both Grandma and Mother used to teach me, even Dad lent a hand. So by the time I started school I was quite prepared and found all subjects fairly easily. I had no trouble with my lessons. My first book was *The Clever Squirrel* by Kulikova. I remember really enjoying it. I read it all by myself and then would retell the story by heart. It took me no more than a few minutes to learn it off by heart .

I liked school. Perhaps the discipline was all we weren't keen on. We had to clean the school yard and premises: we couldn't understand why we had to do the cleaning when we had school cleaners paid to do the job. Yet we had to dust and sweep and clean. Well, we just got on with it.

I recall the time when the new school uniform appeared; we were all told we had to make our new uniform. No more white apron, no more brown dress, now we would wear a three-piece uniform. So some of us made these smart three-piece outfits, the rest continued to wear their old uniform. For some reason the teachers didn't take to the new uniform, so they decided the whole class would wear the old brown dresses with white collar and apron.

I put my foot down: I wouldn't do any more sewing, we'd spent all our money on the change, I would only buy the change of dress if they gave me money to do so. Mother would not give me any more money. So I fell out with our teachers and got a black mark for bad behaviour. But I didn't behave badly on purpose.

Perestroika had no effect on the school, lessons went on as always and our relations with the teachers didn't alter. They permitted no discussion or dispute during lessons! Mother used to go along to all the parent meetings; I cannot recall my father going once, at least no more than once. So it was Mother who went.

When I was nine I joined the October Children, I was ever so thrilled, I had a star pinned on me and was very proud. I felt as if I was a grown-up already. Then I went on to the Young

Pioneers; we had another title, 'Senior Pioneers'; I remember going into a room, the Young Pioneer Room, where we had some sort of special military glory museum. We were told about the wartime history of our Kurgan Region. I remember my induction into the Young Pioneers with much fondness.

I wanted to join the Komsomol because I was fed up having to wear the red Pioneer scarf. I was keen to get rid of it as soon as I could, so as to show how grown up I was, and to wear the Komsomol badge, like all senior formers. I was so eager to be an adult, and when I put on my badge I felt grown up already. So I joined the Komsomol; the ceremony was in the same Pioneer room, though it was more difficult than I thought. There were several people present and we were asked all sorts of questions.

Even when I had to go to the District Communist Party building to get to my Komsomol membership card I was not particularly nervous. They just handed over the card and shook your hand.

I was put in charge of the mass culture sector for my class. A few people were responsible for the work, doing the various tasks given us for the class. We organized games and parties for the smaller children. I found that quite interesting.

When I was at school I wanted to emulate the exploits of the brave partisan girl Zoya Kosmodemyanskaya who fought against the Nazis. When I joined the Komsomol our class bore her name; we had to write down whom we would like to be like. So we all wrote her name. I must say I didn't deep down want to copy her. I just wrote what was expected of me. Now when I have just read Mitchell's *Gone with the Wind*, and recently seen the film, I would probably like to be as strong as the heroine in the book; she managed to overcome all the obstacles in her way.

I was very keen on English at school, I even dreamed of becoming an interpreter one day. So when I was in the last class I asked my parents' advice about going to education college, doing foreign languages.

It was at college that, in 1989, I witnessed the Komsomol disintegrate before my very eyes. It happened all at once, without any meeting, without taking away our membership cards. I still have mine along with other documents. After perestroika we even lost the compulsory job placement.

Nowadays you have to find work yourself after graduation; and if you cannot find any here—and it's a hard search in the city finding a job in your language teaching specialism—you have to go elsewhere. The same principle remains, only you are not forced to leave your home town. But if you want to work you have to go where work is, or simply seek employment in some other area. You suit yourself.

My parents suggested I might get a job where they work, not necessarily in my own field, or maybe with some of our acquaintances. I don't fancy teaching in the schools we have now; all I want to do is teach foreign languages. But in school you have to do a few administrative chores as well. In any case they pay so little. I recall my teaching practice and how tough it all was. Working with one or two people is much simpler and more interesting, distinctly more satisfying.

I am very fond of my parents, but I'd much prefer to live independently. Ideally I'd like to have my own flat, to go off somewhere, so that I am not a perpetual burden on other people. I'd like to test myself as an adult, see how things work out on my own. I don't fancy living off my parents all the time. So my aim is to have my own home. That's what I'd like. Of course, you need money for that—that is, you have to work and find employment for yourself. At the moment I don't know what I am going to do.

I might not stay in Kurgan, maybe I'll take off to another town; I don't want to live in the countryside, though. My parents would love to have their own plot of land in the country—perhaps it's the voice of their ancestors calling. Dad retires this spring, so he is even thinking of buying a cottage and setting himself up there, running a small farmstead. Maybe they will move and leave the flat to me. I'd be delighted.

About Love

My Grandma says she married out of need, not love. That happened in those days: you got married not because you loved someone, but simply because there were too many mouths to feed. When she was 18, they simply married her off. She had absolutely no idea who her husband would be; she had never even set eyes on him before the wedding. The matchmakers just came along and fixed it all up. And Gran accepted her fate meekly. She's still the same, never a cross word about anyone.

She's so easy-going. While Granddad will show his feelings and tear someone off a strip, she simply holds her peace or just tries to calm him down. You'll never hear a cross word out of her; that's how they've lived all these years, with never a thought of divorce.

Mother tells me she married for love, yet there doesn't seem to be any tender feelings between her and Dad these days, it's more like a business relationship.

I've never heard my parents discuss sex, nor have they mentioned it to me. What I have picked up is from friends, books or films. Not that you'd find many books on the subject; all there is would be dog-eared old books. Most of what I know comes from friends.

I don't think you have to get married if you love one another. Marriage won't make you stop loving. You can always help each other in life. What bugs me is that everyone pressures you to register a marriage—otherwise people look down on you. As far as I'm concerned, I would readily agree to live with someone without registering the marriage, if it weren't for my parents. What difference does it make whether you register or not? You can always get up and quit if you feel like it. Of course, we would face other complications. Divorce invariably involves a pile of documents and a whole cartload of papers involved in who owns what. That's even worse.

In my view love and sex are inseparable, although it doesn't always work out that way, no matter how much I personally would like it to. All the same, you can't get far on love alone, especially nowadays. I'd like both sides to live harmoniously and, of course, for them both to have a job. The material side of any partnership also plays a vital part in a relationship. You can't get by without it. I don't think I could get married to someone who is rich but for whom I have no feelings whatsoever. I couldn't last long in such a relationship.

I have no desire to marry a foreigner, as some girls want. I'd like to marry a Russian simply because he would be closer to me; everyone ought to live in their own land. I wouldn't mind working for a while overseas, but I would never go abroad forever. Here I have my friends, my parents, all my relatives, most of whom could never get abroad to see me anyway. That's fate, isn't it?

The Russian Memoirs Series

AT HOME WITH THE GENTRY. A Victorian English lady's diary of Russian country life

attributed to AMELIA LYONS
edited by JOHN MCNAIR

A newly-discovered account of an Englishwoman's extended stay in the province of Tambov in the early 1850s.

ISBN 1 900405 05 9 paper   1998, 153 pages

ARZAMAS-16. The memoirs of a nuclear scientist in the Soviet era

by V. A. TSUKERMAN and Z. M. AZARKH
edited by MICHAEL PURSGLOVE

An insider's view of work in a closed establishment, of life in a Jewish family in Vitebsk in the 1920s, and of Tsukerman's adaptation to developing blindness.

ISBN 1 900405 04 0 paper   forthcoming 1999

Also from Bramcote Press

SCHISM IN HIGH SOCIETY. Lord Radstock and his followers

by Nikolai Leskov
translated and edited by James Muckle

A contemporary account of the English evangelist's campaigns in Russia in the 1870s.

ISBN 0 9517853 5 4 hardback
ISBN 0 9517853 4 6 paper   1995, 128 pages

VALE OF TEARS and 'On Quakeresses'

by Nikolai Leskov
translated by James Muckle

A portrait of the village Russia of Leskov's childhood in the 1840s and an account of the spiritual awakening of the young narrator. A tribute to Quaker famine relief.

ISBN 0 9517853 0 3 paper   1991, 126 pages

DUCK-HUNTING and LAST SUMMER IN CHULIMSK

by Aleksandr Vampilov
translated by Patrick Miles

Acting versions of the dramatist's masterpiece, *Duck-Hunting*, and of his other moving portrait of Russia in decline.

ISBN 0 9517853 3 8 paper   1994, 158 pages

TRADITIONS IN NEW FREEDOM. Christianity and higher education in Russia and Ukraine today

by JONATHAN SUTTON

ISBN 0 9517853 7 0 hardback   1996, 128 pages

RUSSIAN-ENGLISH DICTIONARY OF CONTEMPORARY SLANG. A guide to the living language of today

by 'UFO' (VALERY NIKOLSKI)
second edition edited by JAMES DAVIE

ISBN 1 900405 03 2 paper   1997, 153 pages

ТРАНЗИТ. A bridge to advanced Russian language studies

by DAPHNE WEST and MICHAEL RANSOME

A textbook for learners of Russian at an intermediate stage of language study.

ISBN 1 900405 00 8 paper   1996, 144 pages